SHOCKED
BY THE BIBLE

SHOCKED
BY THE BIBLE

THE MOST ASTONISHING FACTS YOU'VE NEVER BEEN TOLD

JOE KOVACS

W Publishing Group

An Imprint of Thomas Nelson

Published in Nashville, Tennessee, by W Publishing Group, an imprint of Thomas Nelson.

Thomas Nelson titles may be purchased in bulk for educational, business, fund-raising, or sales promotional use. For information, please e-mail SpecialMarkets@ThomasNelson.com.

ISBN: 978-0-7180-9650-2 (trade paper)

Library of Congress Cataloging-in-Publication Data

Kovacs, Joe.
  Shocked by the Bible : the most astonishing facts you've never been told / Joe Kovacs.
    p. cm.
  ISBN 978-0-8499-2011-0 (hardcover)
  1. Bible—Miscellanea. I. Title.
  BS615.K68 2009
  220.6—dc22   2008023042

Printed in the United States of America

16 17 18 19 20 21 RRD 6 5 4 3 2 1

To those seeking the Truth of God

My people are destroyed for lack of knowledge. (Hosea 4:6)

For the time will come when they will not endure sound doctrine . . . And they shall turn away their ears from the truth, and shall be turned unto fables. (2 Timothy 4:3–4)

CONTENTS

I would like to thank my closest friends for their unwavering help and encouragement; the publisher, Thomas Nelson, for having the strength of character to see this project come to fruition; and the countless number of people who have simply been mistaken about what the Bible actually says. The common lack of knowledge helped inspire me to shine a light on the dark, vast ocean of misconceptions.

INTRODUCTION

NO ONE TWISTED my arm; neither did I have a nine-hundred-foot Jesus standing at the foot of my bed, commanding me to write this book under threat of "calling me home." Yet this book needed to be written. There are too many myths and misconceptions about what is in the Bible and what is not. Sadly, lifelong, churchgoing Christians are often as confused as anyone else.

I'd like to make it clear at the outset that this book is *not* about religion or anyone's personal faith. It's about the Bible. While I, myself, am a Christian, I'm not a preacher, and I don't play one on TV.

I happen to write the way I speak, very informally with an occasional attempt at humor. I say "attempt" because I'm also not a professional comedian. I'm just a journalist fed up with the lack of accurate knowledge about what's in the Bible.

My focus is merely to educate about what the Bible says in its own words. There is stunning information included between Genesis and Revelation, but much of it has morphed into misinformation and confusion. Too many people today continue to ask, "You mean, *that's* in the Bible?" or "That's *not* in the Bible?"

I need to provide fair warning, though. This is not one of those typical books that says the same old thing. You know, the same religious titles by the same guys with the same tired themes, like, "It is so awesome to know the *Lord*!" (this last word spoken in two breathy syllables). Or, "This book will grant you peace and understanding in your journey to a blessed life now and in the hereafter. Yada yada yada. Blah, blah, blah."

The Lord is awesome—but enough with the spiritual crystal crunching! If you really hunger and thirst for the truth, and are sick of being in the dark, being misinformed, or worse, being lied to, then keep reading.

Most people are already aware of some famous Bible names and stories, from the parting of the Red Sea to the major miracles of Jesus Christ. Most have heard about Noah's ark, David and Goliath, Peter and Paul, and Jesus changing water into wine. This book does not rehash what you already know. It's meant to startle you with truths you did not know were in Scripture, to get you to think with a new perspective. I'm not talking about trivial names and places no one can pronounce. I am talking about major issues, including who God is, who you are, why you were born, and your ultimate destiny.

The pages are filled with quotations from the King James Version of the Holy Bible, along with a few more modern translations for clarity. I also provide some commentary to help you along. I don't mind if you disagree with my analysis or the humorous manner with which I present some material, but the words of Scripture speak for themselves. You can read along with your own Bible and highlight the verses, but you don't need to have one with you to read this book.

As you read through each chapter, you'll see how different this book really is. It may make you laugh, cry, shout for joy, praise God, argue with Him, shake your head in amazement, condemn the publisher, or do laundry with a new attitude. It may even tick you off to the point where you'll want to "have it out" with those who taught you—or more accurately, did not teach you—the astounding information you'll find here. You may want to ask them why you were kept in the dark. Do they, perhaps, have some sort of agenda in keeping the truth from you? Are they like Jack Nicholson's *A Few Good Men* character who proclaimed, "You can't handle the truth!"?

This book is both for those who have never read the Bible, and those who have been reading it for years and know it well—or at least think they know it well. It's for conservatives, liberals, libertarians, independents, and those who cannot stomach any kind of politics.

Don't worry. You will be able to understand what's written. There's no need to break out a dictionary. The Bible quotes are easy to understand, and if I think there's a chance you might not get them, I provide a variety of translations to highlight the meaning. You don't have to do anything but read.

I recommend reading the chapters in their presented order, but you don't have to. You're an individual, and you have different questions you want answered. Feel free to skip around, but make sure you do eventually read every chapter. You won't regret it.

You'll learn some funny, even silly ideas. But you'll also discover astonishing facts about issues that have perplexed people for ages. Some of what you read may be completely new information; some may be a refresher course. But whatever the case, you'll have no more excuses not to know what the Word of God says. It's time to be *Shocked by the Bible!*

CHAPTER ONE

THE REAL CHRISTMAS STORY

IT'S OFFICIAL. America has gone cuckoo over Christmas! At least it seems that way, with a bizarre culture war raging over December 25. And though it may seem like a recent phenomenon, it's a battle that dates back hundreds of years. The earliest Americans, who were Christians, actually banned the celebration of the day.

At the end of each calendar year, stores, schools, and even some towns struggle over whether or not to publicly display anything associated with the Christmas holiday. The greeting "Merry Christmas" is discouraged, and many places of business replace it with the more generic "Happy Holidays" so as not to offend those who do not take part in the Christmas celebration. Some places remove Christmas trees from public places—Sea-Tac Airport in the state of Washington did so in December 2006.

The political correctness has become so absurd that NBC's *Saturday Night Live* featured a hilarious comedy sketch in December 2005 that showed holiday carolers changing the lyrics of "Silent Night" from "holy night" to "regular night," and "holy infant" to "random infant."

In the skit, comedian Kenan Thompson portrayed NBC personality Al Roker celebrating "holiday time" instead of Christmastime at New York City's Rockefeller Center. The Roker character introduced the "Silent Night" song by saying, "So in the spirit of diversity and fear, please welcome the NBC Peacock Singers with an all-inclusive holiday medley for everyone."

The lyrics stated:

Silent night,
Regular night
All is calm,
All is bright.
Round the fire
Mother and child
Random infant
Religiously neutral
Sleep in comfortable beds
Sleep in comfortable beds.

But the battle lines in this politically correct controversy are not as clear as they seem. There are many different approaches to Christmas.

Some people love every aspect of Christmas, even its name. They regard it as one of the holiest times of the year, and celebrate it in commemoration of the birth of Jesus Christ, the Savior of mankind. For many, it's the one time of year that they attend church. They also enjoy the jolly, secular aspects, from Christmas trees and presents to office parties and holiday revelry.

Some believe the birth of Jesus should be honored on December 25, but think the modern commercialization detracts from the significance of the holy day. They feel the mayhem at the malls makes a mockery of the so-called "reason for the season."

Others love Christmas as a fun-filled time to carouse and exchange gifts, but shy away from the religious aspects, especially in the public arena. They enjoy singing songs, going to parties, and sending cards with winter scenes or messages of "Season's Greetings," but purposefully avoid mentioning God. Some of these folks have been in the news for trying to ban the word *Christmas* or outlaw religious-themed songs and displays in public. In December 2002, a first-grade teacher in Sacramento County, California, said she had been ordered by her principal not to utter the word *Christmas* at school.

Still others enjoy the day as a pagan holiday, the origins of which predate the birth of Jesus by thousands of years. They point to yuletide customs that have nothing to do with the Bible. They often say they are honoring the winter solstice, as the sun begins to lengthen its time each day in the Northern Hemisphere.

Finally, some believe Christmas is completely unchristian, that its pagan origins make it unacceptable in the eyes of the true God, who feels no honor to be associated with traditions tied to the worship of the sun and trees. They point out that the Christians who founded the American colonies made it a crime in some places to celebrate December 25 as a special day, because they believed it was a heathen celebration.

The situation is certainly complex, and there are strong feelings on all sides of the issue. What is Christmas *actually* about? Who is right and who is wrong, or has everyone slid off the right track?

NOT on the Christmas List

To start, none of the following items are mentioned in the Bible concerning the birth of Jesus: the word *Christmas*; a Christmas tree (or any tree, for that matter); hanging ornaments; December; the exact day, date, or even year Jesus was born; three wise men; a little drummer boy; winter; snow; yule; yule logs; wreaths; boughs of holly; mistletoe; colorful lights; eggnog; candy canes; parties; drinking; shopping; reindeer; St. Nick; Santa Claus; elves; toys; wrapping paper; caroling; cookies; plum pudding; chimneys; stockings; colors of red, green, and white; Bing Crosby; Jimmy Stewart; or children coveting a Red Ryder BB gun, despite the fact they may shoot their eyes out as depicted in the film *A Christmas Story*.

I don't think many people will be shocked that Bing Crosby dreaming of a white Christmas and Jimmy Stewart's *It's a Wonderful Life* are absent from the pages of the Bible, but I cannot say the same for some of the other items on this list (which has been checked twice).

For instance, if asked how many wise men were present at the Bethlehem manger when Jesus was born, most people will likely answer, "Three." They would be wrong.

The correct answer from the Bible is actually . . . zero! No Scripture shows the presence of any wise men at the manger at the birth of Jesus. The New Testament indicates the wise men showed up later—*perhaps more than a year later*—at a house in an unspecified location. Of course, those who guess incorrectly are in good company. Even the 2006 film *The Nativity Story* wrongly portrayed a trio of wise men arriving at the manger in Bethlehem.

Interestingly, the holy Scriptures never reveal exactly how many wise men eventually came to visit Jesus. It may have been three, but it could have been four, five, a dozen, or scores. The Bible does not specify. So where did the so-called "Three Wise Men" originate? Christians over the centuries likely assumed there were three because there are three gifts mentioned—gold, frankincense, and myrrh.

The Facts of the Matter

The myth of the "Three Wise Men" raises a serious issue, though. If it isn't contained in Scripture, then what exactly *does* the Bible say about the birth of Jesus?

The accounts are located in the gospels of Matthew and Luke, which do include the following: Mary, Joseph, Jesus, Bethlehem, Nazareth, angelic appearances, a manger, shepherds, wise men, a virgin, a census, a taxation, a despotic ruler, and conception by the Holy Spirit (or as the King James Version calls it, the Holy Ghost).

Before the actual conception and birth of Jesus, an angel conveyed the news to Mary, a virgin engaged to a carpenter named Joseph: "The angel Gabriel was sent from God unto a city of Galilee, named Nazareth, to a virgin espoused to a man whose name was Joseph, of the house of David; and the virgin's name was Mary" (Luke 1:26–27).

Mary was afraid and confused when the angel first greeted her, but the heavenly messenger was quick to explain the good news.

> And the angel said unto her, Fear not, Mary: for thou hast found favour with God. And, behold, thou shalt conceive in thy womb, and bring forth a son, and shalt call his name JESUS. He shall be great, and shall be called the Son of the Highest: and the Lord God shall give unto him the throne of his father David: And he shall reign over the house of Jacob for ever; and of his kingdom there shall be no end. (vv. 30–33)

She confirmed her virtuous state in direct conversation with the angel, as she wondered how she could give birth without having had sexual relations with a man.

> Then said Mary unto the angel, How shall this be, seeing I know not a man? And the angel answered and said unto her, The Holy Ghost shall

come upon thee, and the power of the Highest shall overshadow thee: therefore also that holy thing which shall be born of thee shall be called the Son of God. (vv. 34–35)

Matthew also mentions Mary's virginity, noting that Joseph did not have sex with her until after she had given birth to Jesus: "And [Joseph] knew her not till she had brought forth her firstborn son: and he called his name JESUS" (1:25).

Joseph and Mary were not residents of Bethlehem, the town where Jesus was born. They lived in Nazareth, a city in the region of Galilee. But they were not in Bethlehem because they were homeless wanderers. According to Scripture, they were law-abiding citizens who were following orders to pay their taxes in a census ordered by the Roman authorities.

And it came to pass in those days, that there went out a decree from Caesar Augustus that all the world should be taxed. (And this taxing was first made when Cyrenius was governor of Syria.) And all went to be taxed, every one into his own city. And Joseph also went up from Galilee, out of the city of Nazareth, into Judaea, unto the city of David, which is called Bethlehem; (because he was of the house and lineage of David:) to be taxed with Mary his espoused wife, being great with child. And so it was, that, while they were there, the days were accomplished that she should be delivered. And she brought forth her firstborn son, and wrapped him in swaddling clothes, and laid him in a manger; because there was no room for them in the inn. (Luke 2:1–7)

The Son of God entered the world in a manger not because His parents couldn't afford accommodations but because there was no vacancy at the "Bethlehem Inn." Many people were traveling due to the census, so finding lodging was more difficult than usual.

As an aside, it's interesting that Jesus was not an only child. He had at least four brothers mentioned by name and at least two unnamed sisters, as Matthew reveals later: "Is not this the carpenter's son? Is not his mother called Mary? and his brethren, James, and Joses, and Simon, and Judas? And his sisters, are they not all with us?" (13:55–56)

The Season Ain't the Reason

But back to the birth of Jesus in the Bethlehem manger, according to Luke's account: "And there were in the same country shepherds abiding in the field, keeping watch over their flock by night" (2:8).

While we're never told precisely what season it was when Jesus was born, some use this verse to suggest that it was either spring, summer, or fall, but not winter. They argue that the winter months are too cold and wet for shepherds in Israel to be in the fields at night. In this view, October would likely have been the latest month for them to have their flocks out. But the Bible is silent on the season.

> And, lo, the angel of the Lord came upon them, and the glory of the Lord shone round about them: and they were sore afraid. And the angel said unto them, Fear not: for, behold, I bring you good tidings of great joy, which shall be to all people. For unto you is born this day in the city of David a Saviour, which is Christ the Lord. And this shall be a sign unto you; ye shall find the babe wrapped in swaddling clothes, lying in a manger. And suddenly there was with the angel a multitude of the heavenly host praising God, and saying, Glory to God in the highest, and on earth peace, good will toward men. (vv. 9–14)

Many people who celebrate Christmas are familiar with at least some of these six verses, as they often appear as inspirational messages on Christmas cards. The shepherds were terrified as they experienced a miraculous appearance from the unseen world. They saw not just one angel but a large number of heavenly messengers praising God.

> And it came to pass, as the angels were gone away from them into heaven, the shepherds said one to another, Let us now go even unto Bethlehem, and see this thing which is come to pass, which the Lord hath made known unto us. And they came with haste, and found Mary, and Joseph, and the babe lying in a manger. And when they had seen it, they made known abroad the saying which was told them concerning this child. And all they that heard it wondered at those things which were told them by the shepherds. But Mary kept all these things, and pondered them in

her heart. And the shepherds returned, glorifying and praising God for all the things that they had heard and seen, as it was told unto them. And when eight days were accomplished for the circumcising of the child, his name was called JESUS, which was so named of the angel before he was conceived in the womb. (vv. 15–21)

According to Luke, the shepherds who received angelic instructions hurried into Bethlehem, found the baby in the manger, and then returned to their fields, all the while praising God. Again, there is no mention of any wise men at the manger. Neither are they mentioned in the first eight days of Jesus' life, when He was circumcised and given His name.

The first mention of the wise men is in the second chapter of Matthew. They arrived sometime after Jesus was born, but it's not clear precisely when. Because they were not certain of the exact place of birth, they sought help from the local ruler:

Now when Jesus was born in Bethlehem of Judaea in the days of Herod the king, behold, there came wise men from the east to Jerusalem, saying, Where is he that is born King of the Jews? for we have seen his star in the east, and are come to worship him. When Herod the king had heard these things, he was troubled, and all Jerusalem with him. And when he had gathered all the chief priests and scribes of the people together, he demanded of them where Christ should be born. And they said unto him, In Bethlehem of Judaea: for thus it is written by the prophet, And thou Bethlehem, in the land of Juda, art not the least among the princes of Juda: for out of thee shall come a Governor, that shall rule my people Israel. Then Herod, when he had privily called the wise men, enquired of them diligently what time the star appeared. And he sent them to Bethlehem, and said, Go and search diligently for the young child; and when ye have found him, bring me word again, that I may come and worship him also. (vv. 2:1–8)

The Starring Role

As the wise men searched for the Christ child, they received miraculous help from a star acting as a global positioning device: "When they had heard the king, they departed; and, lo, the star, which they saw in the east, went before them, till it came and stood over where the young child was. When they saw the star, they rejoiced with exceeding great joy" (vv. 9–10).

There are different theories about the star in these verses. Some say it was an actual star. Others claim it was a planetary conjunction, which creates a very bright light in the sky. Still others suggest it was an angel guiding them to the right place, since the text notes that the star moved, and other verses of the Bible refer to angels as stars (see Job 38:4–7 and Revelation 1:15–20).

But whatever they followed to get there, when the wise men finally gazed upon Jesus, it was not in a manger but in a *house*: "And when they were come into the house, they saw the young child with Mary his mother, and fell down, and worshipped him" (Matthew 2:11).

The wise men were then warned by God in a dream not to return to King Herod, so they returned to their homeland by another route. Herod finally realized the Magi were not returning, and he became so angry that he slaughtered an entire generation of young boys in and around Bethlehem.

Then Herod, when he saw that he was mocked of the wise men, was exceeding wroth, and sent forth, and slew all the children that were in Bethlehem, and in all the coasts thereof, from two years old and under, according to the time which he had diligently inquired of the wise men. (v. 16)

There is an important point here: according to what he had learned from the Magi about the time of Jesus' birth, Herod slew boys up to two years old. That means it's possible the wise men found Jesus up to two years after He was born! Remember, they were not present at the manger. They arrived later at a *house* to present their gifts. It could have been the day after He was born, but it's also possible baby Jesus was no longer a baby when they arrived. He may have been walking and talking. Additionally, while Luke's account refers to Jesus in the manger as a "babe," all seven references in the gospel of Matthew (the account mentioning the wise men) refer to Him as a "young child," coming from a different Greek word than the one translated "babe."

After the wise men left, Joseph and Mary were warned about the coming slaughter and told by an angel to flee to Egypt. They did so, and returned to Israel only after Herod was dead.

That is the extent of the gospel accounts of the birth of Jesus. They contain a lot less than what has been floating around, as they clearly lack many of the fables that have become a cottage industry for merchants. There are no chestnuts roasting on an open fire, no "Jingle Bell Rock," and no one's grandma got run over by a reindeer. Throughout the remainder of the New Testament, there are no accounts of birthday celebrations for Jesus, either during His life or after His death and resurrection. If the apostles ever celebrated it, it's not mentioned in any book of the Bible.

The Coca-Cola Connection

As for the customs people associate with Christmas today, some are very new, while others date back to antiquity from religions other than Christianity.

Among the newer customs is the image of Santa Claus, aka Father Christmas or St. Nick (not to be confused with Old Nick, which is another name for the devil). The chubby, white-bearded man in a red and white suit is the result of an evolution of sketches and descriptions from the late 1800s. Ironically, the character was not always depicted as an obese old man, but appeared younger and elflike in some illustrations. The image of an old, fat man in his red and white outfit received a great deal of help from a Coca-Cola marketing campaign in the early twentieth century. The company wanted to remind people that Coke was not just a summertime beverage, so in 1922 it employed the slogan "Thirst Knows No Season." Nine years later, the soda giant used drawings by Michigan-born illustrator Haddon Sundblom to spread the jolly look of the fat man worldwide.

Santa Claus's other name, Kris Kringle, shows how Christianity intermixed with fiction. Kris Kringle derives from the word *Christkindl*, which is German for "Christ child." It's astonishing that Jesus Christ of Nazareth, the Christ child, has morphed into Kris Kringle, aka Santa Claus.

Banned in the USA

Despite the assumptions of many, Christmas was not a widespread holiday in colonial America. In the seventeenth and eighteenth centuries, settlers in New England did not celebrate it. Shocking as it sounds, followers of Jesus Christ in both America and England helped pass laws making it illegal to observe Christmas, believing it was an insult to God to honor a day associated with ancient paganism. Most Americans today are unaware that Christmas was banned in Boston from 1659 to 1681.

Additionally, on December 25, 1789, the first Christmas under the new U.S. Constitution, Congress was in session. Whether or not the politicians were actually hard at work is another story. Christmas was not declared a federal holiday until 1870.

Christmas Customs Before Jesus

Enter the words *Christmas, pagan,* and *origin* into any online search engine, and a startling truth will emerge. Many customs surrounding Christmas date back thousands of years, even long *before* Jesus Christ was born in Bethlehem.

Most historians mention the ancient practice of honoring the sun god in late December, as the days began to lengthen after the annual winter solstice. In ancient Rome, the time of year was known as *Dies Natalis Invicti Solis,* which in English means "the Birthday of the Unconquered Sun." Parties, banquets, and gift exchanges were held in late December for the festival known as Saturnalia, named for the heathen god Saturn. Over the centuries, these celebrations of heathen gods mixed with the worship of the true Son of God, and customs not endorsed by the Bible became intertwined with the spread of Christianity.

Does God Hate Christmas Trees?

As an example of such a custom, consider the Christmas tree. There is no mention of it in the pages of Scripture. The wise men did not put their gifts under a tree adorned with silver tinsel and gold garland and then wait with breathless anticipation. Not surprisingly, few people today who put Christmas trees in their homes understand exactly where the tradition comes from, or can provide scriptural reasons for having them.

However, there *is* an ancient custom cited in the Old Testament that involves trees. The tradition is hauntingly similar to modern Christmas trees, and is strongly condemned by God, who urges His people to avoid the custom. As the prophet Jeremiah wrote:

> Thus saith the LORD, Learn not the way of the heathen, and be not dismayed at the signs of heaven; for the heathen are dismayed at them. For the customs of the people are vain: for one cutteth a tree out of the forest,

the work of the hands of the workman, with the axe. They deck it with silver and with gold; they fasten it with nails and with hammers, that it move not. They are upright as the palm tree, but speak not: they must needs be borne, because they cannot go. Be not afraid of them; for they cannot do evil, neither also is it in them to do good. (10:2–5)

It's extremely rare for anyone to hear these verses preached or discussed in Christian churches, especially during the month of December.

Jeremiah is thought to have written his book between 627 and 560 BC, more than five hundred years *before* Jesus was born in Bethlehem. The verses indicate this tree-decorating custom was a heathen practice and followed by people who worshipped nonexistent gods. The customs are specifically called "vain," which stems from the Hebrew word *hebel,* which means "breath" or "vapor," and "vain," "vanity," or "worthless." In fact, the NIV Bible translates the King James word *vain* as "worthless": "For the customs of the peoples are worthless" (v. 3).

The text gives some detail about the custom, stating it involves chopping down a tree with an axe, and shaping or "trimming" the tree. The pagan worshippers would tie it up so it would not sway or fall, and they would "deck" it with silver and gold. It's interesting to note the King James transla-tion of the Bible uses the word *deck,* clearly reminiscent of the famous Christmas carol "Deck the Halls."

Scripture goes on to state that people should not be afraid of the items, "for they cannot do evil, neither also is it in them to do good" (v. 5). That just points out the obvious. They are simply trees, hunks of wood that can be chopped down and thrown into a fire. Nevertheless, God explicitly stated, *"Learn not the way of the heathen."*

In other verses, the Bible records God's displeasure with His own people for following such tree-related worship practices in groves. For example:

And the children of Israel did evil in the sight of the LORD, and forgat the LORD their God, and served Baalim and the groves. (Judges 3:7)

For the LORD shall smite Israel . . . because they have made their groves, provoking the LORD to anger. (1 Kings 14:15)

For they also built them high places, and images, and groves, on every high hill, and under every green tree. (1 Kings 14:23)

Give Us a Kiss

What about the mistletoe? Why do people kiss under it? Did Mary and Joseph kiss under mistletoe in the Bible? The question may seem ridiculous, but most people do not know that the practice of hanging mistletoe and seeking to kiss or be kissed beneath it are ancient pagan customs.

Mistletoe was revered by pagans for its fertility. It not only bloomed in the dark months of winter, but ancient Druids reportedly believed it to be the sperm of the forest gods, as its berries contain a liquid that bears a striking resemblance to human semen. Hence, the practice of kissing underneath it.

There are other Christmas customs we have adopted from pagan traditions too. For example, the holiday colors of red, green, and white were sacred to Druids. The word *yule* is an ancient reference to the winter solstice, when heathens burned yule logs in honor of the pagan god of the same name. Many people eat a traditional Christmas ham, yet remain unaware that ancient heathens ate a pig on December 25 in honor of the Norse god Frey, who in mythology rode a boar.

Some modern pagans, such as Wiccan high priestess Selena Fox of Circle Sanctuary in Wisconsin, even suggest that people today should reclaim Santa Claus as a pagan god by decorating him with images reminiscent of his various heritages, ranging from the Greek god Cronos (also known as Father Time) to Odin, the Scandinavian Allfather, who travels across the sky on an eight-legged horse.

No doubt the list of holiday customs will only increase in the future. But for now, a more complete picture of the real Christmas story has been unwrapped.

CHAPTER TWO

THE DAY JESUS DIED

HOLY SMOKES! Can you believe the Bible never specifically says that Jesus Christ died on a Friday? For that matter, can you believe the Bible never says Jesus rose at sunrise on a Sunday morning?

Stunning as it sounds, both are true, and you are about to see it for yourself.

"But everyone, believers and nonbelievers alike, knows how the story goes. Jesus died on a Friday afternoon and rose on Sunday morning!"

I hear ya. I've also listened to that claim my entire life. It's a popular tale, a virtual no-brainer. For hundreds of years, people have lived under the impression that Jesus Christ was crucified on a Friday afternoon, laid in the grave Friday evening, and rose from the dead around sunrise on Sunday morning.

The Bible *does* say Jesus died and rose from the dead. There is absolutely no disputing that. But the actual timeline of these events is less clear. While the Gospels provide some details, they don't name the precise day of the week or date of the crucifixion, and they're astonishingly silent on the exact moment of resurrection.

So what day *did* Jesus die? Nearly everyone has heard the phrase "Good Friday," as millions believe Christ was crucified on Friday. Many accept it as a fact. But the word *Friday* does not appear in the Bible; nor does *Sunday*. Even if it's just a matter of semantics, the Bible never says Jesus died on a

Friday or rose Sunday morning. That doesn't mean the Scriptures are silent about the issue, though. If they're read closely, they do provide clues about which day Jesus died.

In the ancient world, most days of the week in Scripture did not have special names. They were simply referred to by a number.

When God first delineated the days at Creation, we read:

And God called the light Day, and the darkness he called Night. And the evening and the morning were the first day. (Genesis 1:5)

And the evening and the morning were the second day. (v. 8)

And the evening and the morning were the third day. (v. 13)

The only day of the week designated with a special name is the seventh day of the week, which is called the Sabbath, meaning "day of rest." It is the equivalent of Saturday in our modern calendar: "And on the seventh day God ended his work which he had made; and he rested on the seventh day from all his work which he had made. And God blessed the seventh day, and sanctified it: because that in it he had rested from all his work which God created and made" (Genesis 2:2–3).

Not only does it hark all the way back to the first week of Creation in Genesis, but it's also featured in great detail as the fourth commandment:

Remember the sabbath day, to keep it holy. Six days shalt thou labour, and do all thy work: But the seventh day is the sabbath of the LORD thy God: in it thou shalt not do any work, thou, nor thy son, nor thy daughter, thy manservant, nor thy maidservant, nor thy cattle, nor thy stranger that is within thy gates: For in six days the LORD made heaven and earth, the sea, and all that in them is, and rested the seventh day: wherefore the LORD blessed the sabbath day, and hallowed it. (Exodus 20:8–11)

For thousands of years, God's people—including Jesus—observed this day of rest by not working on Saturday, and many of their descendants continue the Sabbath tradition today.

In addition, dozens of languages still call "Saturday" their own version of the word *sabbath*. In Greek, it is *sabbaton*; in Italian, *sabato*; Spanish, *sábado*; Russian, *subbota*; Hebrew, *shabbat*; Polish, *sobota*; and Hungarian, *szómbat*.

Why, then, do most people assume Jesus died on a Friday? The simple answer is that Friday is the day before Saturday, and Scripture contains verses suggesting Jesus was put to death the day before a Sabbath.

And that day was the preparation, and the sabbath drew on. (Luke 23:54)

And now when the even was come, because it was the preparation, that is, the day before the Sabbath . . . (Mark 15:42)

After spending six hours being crucified, according to Matthew and Mark, Jesus died at the "ninth hour" of the day, which scholars believe is about 3 p.m., some nine hours after sunrise.

Thus, according to adherents to this timeline, Jesus died on a Friday afternoon around three o'clock. Case closed. But is it, really?

There are problems with the Friday theory. One is the often-overlooked fact that according to the New Testament, there were very likely *two Sabbath days* during the week Jesus died. The Bible mentions a special, *additional* day of rest that week.

The gospel of John takes note of this other Sabbath, which is different from the normal day of rest, Saturday. Break out your Bible highlighters for this one:

When Jesus therefore had received the vinegar, he said, It is finished: and he bowed his head, and gave up the ghost. The Jews therefore, because it was the preparation, that the bodies should not remain upon the cross on the sabbath day, (for that sabbath day was an high day,) besought Pilate that their legs might be broken, and that they might be taken away. (19:30–31)

John went out of his way to be sure readers know this Sabbath was not a typical Saturday Sabbath. He explained it was a "high day." The phrase "high day" refers to the high holy days (holidays, if you will) mentioned in the Old Testament. These were annual Sabbaths in addition to the weekly day of rest.

The Day of Atonement (Leviticus 16:30), Feast of Trumpets (Numbers 29:1), and Feast of Tabernacles (Leviticus 23:34) in the autumn months and the Feast of Unleavened Bread (Exodus 12:17) in spring are all examples of these annual Sabbaths. And just as our annual holidays such as New Year's Day or the Fourth of July can fall on any day of the week, so can these annual high holy days. Of course, these annual Sabbaths have a one-in-seven chance of falling on a regular Sabbath, but that leaves a six-in-seven chance that they would be on any other day of the week.

There is no mystery when this "high day" or annual Sabbath mentioned by John occurred, as Jesus Himself made reference to it:

Now the feast of unleavened bread drew nigh, which is called the Passover. (Luke 22:1)

And they went, and found as he had said unto them: and they made ready the passover. And when the hour was come, he sat down, and the twelve apostles with him. And he said unto them, With desire I have desired to eat this passover with you before I suffer. (Luke 22:13–15)

The New Living Translation is more direct. It says explicitly that this "high day" was in Passover week: "The Jewish leaders didn't want the victims hanging there the next day, which was the Sabbath (and a very special Sabbath at that, because it was the Passover), so they asked Pilate to hasten their deaths by ordering that their legs be broken. Then their bodies could be taken down" (John 19:31).

This means the famous Last Supper, as it has come to be known, was a Passover meal.

As we just read, Jesus Himself said, "With desire I have desired to eat this passover with you before I suffer."

Even in the years after Jesus' death, Paul equated the Son of God with the Passover celebration: "For even Christ our passover is sacrificed for us" (1 Corinthians 5:7).

The day after Passover is a "high day" Sabbath. It's the first day of the Feast of Unleavened Bread, when believers enjoy a special day of rest and eat unleavened bread.

To recap, Jesus was slain the day before a Sabbath, which was an annual

Sabbath, and there is no mention of "Friday." But are there any other clues in the pages of Scripture to help identify the correct timeline?

Three Days and Three Nights

In the gospel of Matthew, Jesus proved His Messiahship when He predicted the amount of time He would be buried. "For as Jonah was in the belly of the great fish for three days and three nights, so I, the Son of Man, will be in the heart of the earth for three days and three nights" (12:40 NLT).

Many translations mention "three days and three nights." But this raises an interesting question: If Jesus died on a Friday afternoon and rose from the dead on Sunday morning, how is it possible to cram "three days and three nights" into that time period? It's not. It's like an obese person trying to squeeze into a skimpy swimsuit; the results are not pretty, to say the least.

Friday night and Saturday night are two nights. Daytime Saturday is one day. Simply put, there are not three days and three nights. In the commonly accepted theory, there is only half of that.

Jesus was already gone from the tomb when Sunday morning broke. In order to save the idea that Jesus died on Friday and rose on Sunday, some scholars count Sunday morning and Friday afternoon as partial days, and suggest Jesus meant "parts of three days and three nights." Some analysts claim the phrase identifying the three days was actually a Greek idiom that may have meant "parts of three days and three nights," thus allowing for the Friday-through-Sunday time frame. But Jesus was quoting a verse from the book of Jonah, which was written in Hebrew, a completely different language.

Here is the Old Testament story Jesus was quoting: "Now the LORD had prepared a great fish to swallow up Jonah. And Jonah was in the belly of the fish three days and three nights" (Jonah 1:17).

Indeed, Jonah spent three days and three nights inside a fish, and Jesus said he would be in the ground for the same time period, not merely parts of three days and three nights.

This matters, of course, since Scripture is not clear on which day Jesus died. Examining the number of days He said He would be in the earth is crucial to determining whether He died on Friday or not. Perhaps considering the question from the standpoint of the resurrection will help.

As strange as it sounds, the Bible is silent on the exact time Jesus rose from the grave. There were no eyewitnesses to the event. The New Testament simply records that women came to Jesus' tomb on the first day of the week, Sunday: "In the end of the sabbath, as it began to dawn toward the first day of the week, came Mary Magdalene and the other Mary to see the sepulchre" (Matthew 28:1).

We know for sure that the Sabbath mentioned in this verse is the weekly Saturday day of rest (as opposed to the annual high holy day Sabbath), since the Sabbath was ending and dawn was breaking toward the first day of the week.

A Tomb With a View

But did the resurrection take place at the moment the women arrived? No. It happened some time earlier.

> And, behold, there was a great earthquake: for the angel of the Lord descended from heaven, and came and rolled back the stone from the door, and sat upon it . . . And the angel answered and said unto the women, Fear not ye: for I know that ye seek Jesus, which was crucified. He is not here: for he is risen, as he said. Come, see the place where the Lord lay. (Matthew 28:2–6)

The passage does not say Jesus rose from the dead at that instant. In fact, it points out that He was already gone, while an angel rolled back the stone so the women could see the tomb was empty. "He is not here: for he is risen, as he said," they were told. Jesus had risen from the dead at some point *before* their arrival. But the Bible does not say precisely when the tremendous event occurred.

In Luke's account, the women were provided a little more information from the angel: "He is not here, but is risen: remember how he spake unto you when he was yet in Galilee, saying, The Son of Man must be delivered into the hands of sinful men, and be crucified, and the third day rise again" (24:6–7).

The phrase "the third day" can be taken two ways. It can mean He was to rise at any time on the third calendar day. For some, this suggests a Friday death and Sunday resurrection. But the phrase can also indicate the third completed day, or a full seventy-two hours. Again, the Bible is unclear.

Because Jesus was already gone from the grave Sunday morning, assume for the moment that he rose at six o'clock Saturday evening. If He remained in the ground a full "three days and three nights" as He predicted, then He was buried on Wednesday evening. That would mean the "high day" Sabbath mentioned in the gospel of John would have been Thursday. If He were crucified Wednesday afternoon and put in the grave at six o'clock Wednesday evening and rose from the dead at six o'clock Saturday night, then that would be seventy-two hours "in the heart of the earth," exactly three days and three nights. It also matches the teaching from Jesus that He would rise "after three days" (Mark 8:31). When the women arrived early Sunday morning, they discovered the empty tomb.

Supporting this seventy-two-hour theory is another piece of evidence that suggests there were two Sabbath days that week instead of just the usual Saturday. Here's what Luke recounts about the day Jesus died:

> And that day was the preparation, and the sabbath drew on. And the women also, which came with him from Galilee, followed after, and beheld the sepulchre, and how his body was laid. And they returned, and prepared spices and ointments; and rested the sabbath day according to the commandment . . . Now upon the first day of the week, very early in the morning, they came unto the sepulchre, bringing the spices which they had prepared, and certain others with them. And they found the stone rolled away from the sepulchre. (23:54 56; 24:1 2)

Luke notes that the women looked upon Jesus' body as it was being laid in the tomb. At some point after that, they prepared spices and ointments, and rested on the Sabbath day. Then, on the first day of the week (Sunday), they came back to the tomb with the spices they had previously prepared.

Compare the scenario in the gospel of Mark:

> And when the sabbath was past, Mary Magdalene, and Mary the mother of James, and Salome, had bought sweet spices, that they might come and anoint him. And very early in the morning the first day of the week, they came unto the sepulchre at the rising of the sun. (16:1–2)

Mark's picture is very different. The spices were purchased when the Sabbath was finished. But Luke's account suggests the spices were in the women's possession *before* they rested on the Sabbath. Luke had stated, "They returned, and prepared spices and ointments; and rested the sabbath day according to the commandment."

Luke shows the women preparing the spices and ointments *before* the Sabbath, but Mark indicates the women did not buy them until *after* the Sabbath. How was this possible? How could they prepare the spices if they did not have them in their possession? Is it perhaps an error in the Bible? Not if the two-Sabbath theory is correct.

If Jesus died on a Wednesday, the high Sabbath was on Thursday, and the regular Sabbath was on Saturday, then the Gospels are harmonious. The Sabbath that Mark refers to is the annual Sabbath. The women waited until Thursday's day of rest was completed before they bought spices on Friday. According to Luke, they spent Friday preparing these goods, and then rested on the second Sabbath that week, which was Saturday. Finally, on Sunday morning, they went to the tomb and discovered Jesus was gone.

The two-Sabbath theory has people carefully examining Matthew 28:1. The verse in the King James Version reads, "In the end of the sabbath, as it began to dawn toward the first day of the week, came Mary Magdalene and the other Mary to see the sepulchre."

In the original Greek, the word translated as "sabbath" is actually *plural*, as in "Sabbaths." The verse should be rendered, "In the end of the sabbaths," referring to *both* days of rest that week.

Those who steadfastly believe Jesus was executed on a Friday often point to a comment from one of Jesus' disciples on the same Sunday the women discovered the empty tomb. Jesus appeared to a pair of disciples who were discussing the amazing events that had taken place that week, but God did not allow them to recognize Jesus.

The disciple named Cleopas noted, "To day is the third day since these things were done" (Luke 24:21).

Proponents of the "Friday theory" say if the Messiah did die on a Wednesday, and they were speaking about it on Sunday, then Cleopas should have said, "Today is the *fourth* day since these things were done." Ironically, had Jesus died on a Friday, Sunday would only be the second day "since these things were done."

Yet there is a simple explanation. The words "these things" and the actions of "the chief priests and rulers" indicate the disciples had been discussing the important events from the past few days.

And they talked together of all these things which had happened . . . And how the chief priests and our rulers delivered him to be condemned to death, and have crucified him. But we trusted that it had been he which should have redeemed Israel: and beside all this, to day is the third day since these things were done. (Luke 24:14, 20–21)

The events covered by "all these things" did not end the moment Jesus died, since the chief priests and rulers acted again the following day, on Thursday. The gospel of Matthew specifies the rest of "these things."

Now the next day, that followed the day of the preparation, the chief priests and Pharisees came together unto Pilate, saying, Sir, we remember that that deceiver said, while he was yet alive, After three days I will rise again. Command therefore that the sepulchre be made sure until the third day, lest his disciples come by night, and steal him away, and say unto the people, He is risen from the dead: so the last error shall be worse than the first. Pilate said unto them, Ye have a watch: go your way, make it as sure as ye can. So they went, and made the sepulchre sure, sealing the stone, and setting a watch. (27:62–66)

Thus, the rulers sought a guarantee on Thursday that nothing would happen to the body of the man just executed. According to a Wednesday-crucifixion timetable, the main events were completed on Thursday with the sealing of the tomb and posting of the guards, making Sunday "the third day since these things were done."

The Gospel That's Not "Gospel"

To be fair, some people familiar with Scripture will point to one verse near the end of the gospel of Mark that may seem to suggest Jesus rose on the first day of the week, Sunday: "Now when Jesus was risen early the first day of the week, he appeared first to Mary Magdalene, out of whom he had cast seven devils" (16:9).

The biggest question with this verse is: Does it really even exist in the original Word of God? Most translations produced after the King James of 1611 have an important note from experts and Bible commentators who explain that the earliest and most reliable New Testament manuscripts do not even contain Mark 16:9–20. Those twelve verses are not present in the authentic documents. The gospel of Mark might actually conclude at 16:8. The demands of intellectual honesty require confidence that the verses were meant to be in the original Bible and were not added hundreds of years later.

But even if Mark 16:9 in the King James Version is authentic, there is still a reply possible for adherents of the Wednesday theory. First, the passage doesn't say Jesus rose early on the first day of the week. It specifically says He "was risen." To point out the obvious, if He had been resurrected Saturday night, then of course He "was risen" on Sunday. Secondly, there are no commas in the Greek text from which this sentence was translated. Moving the comma in English to another place produces a considerably different meaning. For instance, put the comma after the word *risen*: "Now when Jesus was risen, early the first day of the week he appeared first to Mary Magdalene, out of whom he had cast seven devils."

The verse is now focusing not on when Jesus arose but rather when He made His first appearance.

This variation to the traditional "Friday to Sunday" scenario can be a bit mind-boggling. But what difference does it make, since the important facts are that Jesus died and rose again?

Unfortunately, what many people assume is in the Bible is not always there. This chapter demonstrates, however, that it is possible to read Scripture without any preconceived notions and discover what Scripture actually states. The Bible does not say Jesus died on a Friday or rose Sunday morning. If that really were the case, then Jesus Christ would have been incorrect (or as some nonbelievers suggest, lying) in twice using the phrase "three days and three nights" as the sign proving His true identity as God. Jesus died on a Wednesday, and just as He taught, rose from the dead "after three days" on a Saturday.

CHAPTER THREE

EASTER VANISHED!

LADIES AND GENTLEMEN, Easter has vanished! And the American Civil Liberties Union and atheists had nothing to do with it!

Easter has disappeared from today's Bibles, hopping right off the pages of the New Testament. It has been virtually impossible to find in the four hundred years since the King James Bible made its debut in 1611.

Is it some sort of trick, like a magician making a rabbit disappear? Or is there a sinister plot afoot to bounce what many feel is the "holiest day of the Christian calendar" out of existence? Is the word *Easter* even of Christian origin? And did it originally have anything to do with the resurrection of Jesus, as millions assume? The answers are astounding.

The word *Easter* is found in Scripture, but only once, and almost exclusively in the King James Version. Here's the only mention:

> Now about that time Herod the king stretched forth his hands to vex certain of the church. And he killed James the brother of John with the sword. And because he saw it pleased the Jews, he proceeded further to take Peter also. (Then were the days of unleavened bread.) And when he had apprehended him, he put him in prison, and delivered him to four quaternions of soldiers to keep him; intending after Easter to bring him forth to the people. (Acts 12:1–4)

In translation after translation written since 1611, the word *Easter* has vanished. I examined twenty-five translations and came up Easterless in all but one: the 21st Century King James Version, which is almost a carbon copy of the original. It's absent from well-known Bibles such as the New King James, the American Standard Version, the New International Version, the New American Standard Version, the Good News Bible, and the Amplified Bible.

Did the Rabbit Die?

How did this come about? Did someone take a giant eraser and delete Easter from Scripture? The simple solution to the puzzle lies in the fact that the Bible was not originally written in English. The New Testament documents translated into English are in Greek, and the word that was rendered as "Easter" in Acts 12:4 has nothing to do with the resurrection of Jesus or any celebration of such.

The Greek word in question is *pascha*, and it refers to Passover, not Easter. *Pascha* is used twenty-eight other times in the pages of the New Testament, and the King James Version renders it as "Passover" everywhere except Acts 12:4. The word was apparently mistranslated in that one verse. Since then, other linguists have recognized the error from the seventeenth century and have correctly translated the word as "Passover." Thus, the word *Easter* is no longer found in the pages of modern Bible translations.

Passover is the annual commemoration God instituted on the fourteenth evening of the first month of each Hebrew year (Leviticus 23:5). It was a meal with a main course of roasted lamb, the blood of which was symbolic of God rescuing His people from the death He inflicted on the Egyptians (Exodus 12:12–14). In the Old Testament, God said He would "pass over" the houses of the Israelites. Wherever God saw the blood of slain lambs painted on the front door, He allowed the people to live. But if there was no blood, the firstborn of everything in Egypt, humans as well as animals, was executed by the Lord.

Jesus Himself celebrated the Passover meal during His earthly ministry. Remember, the Last Supper was actually a Passover meal. Leonardo da Vinci could have titled his famous painting *The Last Passover* instead of *The Last Supper*. As mentioned before, many Christians today regard Jesus as the true Passover, with the apostle Paul calling Him "Christ our passover": "For even

Christ our passover is sacrificed for us: Therefore let us keep the feast" (1 Corinthians 5:7–8).

The Bunny Trail

But while the mystery of Easter's disappearance from Scripture has been solved, other questions remain. What does "Easter" mean, anyway? Is it a Christian word? And did the apostles celebrate it?

This may come as a surprise, but the origin of the word *Easter* has nothing to do with the death or resurrection of Jesus. Easter is the name of a pagan goddess of fertility and the dawn that predates Christianity by thousands of years. This ancient Babylonian goddess Ishtar (which some say is pronounced the same as Easter is today) was known by a variety of similar names in other languages and cultures: Astarte to the Phoenicians, Ashtaroth or Ashtoreth to the ancient Israelites, Ostara to the Germans, and Eostre or Eastre to the Anglo-Saxons.

She had nothing to do with the correct worship of the true God. In fact, following the customs associated with this pagan Easter (no matter what name she was known by in any of the various languages) was strongly condemned by the God of the Bible, who referred to her as an "abomination."

Consider the following examples from Scripture. Keep in mind Easter was also called Ashtaroth or Ashtoreth:

And they forsook the LORD, and served Baal and Ashtaroth. (Judges 2:13)

And the children of Israel did evil again in the sight of the LORD, and served Baalim, and Ashtaroth, and the gods of Syria, and the gods of Zidon, and the gods of Moab, and the gods of the children of Ammon, and the gods of the Philistines, and forsook the LORD, and served not him. (Judges 10:6)

And Samuel spake unto all the house of Israel, saying, If ye do return unto the LORD with all your hearts, then put away the strange gods and Ashtaroth from among you, and prepare your hearts unto the LORD, and serve him only: and he will deliver you out of the hand of the Philistines. (1 Samuel 7:3)

And they cried unto the LORD, and said, We have sinned, because we have forsaken the LORD, and have served Baalim and Ashtaroth: but now deliver us out of the hand of our enemies, and we will serve thee. (1 Samuel 12:10)

For Solomon went after Ashtoreth the goddess of the Zidonians, and after Milcom the abomination of the Ammonites. (1 Kings 11:5)

And the high places that were before Jerusalem, which were on the right hand of the mount of corruption, which Solomon the king of Israel had builded for Ashtoreth the abomination of the Zidonians, and for Chemosh the abomination of the Moabites, and for Milcom the abomination of the children of Ammon, did the king defile. (2 Kings 23:13)

The Bible makes it clear God's chosen people did evil in His sight by following customs associated with this abominable, pagan goddess (who does not even really exist).

Because Easter (Ashtoreth) was the goddess of fertility, the customs associated with her naturally had to do with the celebration of fertility and rapidly giving birth. What better symbols could be found than bunnies and eggs?

The Apostles Never Hunted Easter Eggs

Think about it for a moment. What do bunny rabbits and eggs have in common? After all, rabbits don't plop out eggs, as chickens do. They have baby bunnies at a rapid rate. Eggs, of course, are part of the reproduction process. That is why people today decorate eggs. They signify fertility, not the death and resurrection of Jesus.

There is no record in Scripture of the apostles of Jesus ever celebrating Easter as we know it today. When Jesus rose from the dead, His followers did not find a basket of eggs or a chocolate bunny in the empty tomb. There was no rabbit when Jesus made His appearances that Sunday. The apostles did not decorate eggs every March or April. They didn't hide eggs or go on Easter egg hunts throughout the ancient world as they spread the gospel. In fact, the words *egg* and *eggs* appear in the King James translation only nine times, none of which relate to the story of the resurrection of Jesus.

It was not until hundreds of years after the crucifixion and resurrection of Jesus that the fertility customs associated with the pagan goddess Easter firmly mixed with Christianity. As Christianity spread, many new converts to the teachings of Jesus did not abandon their heathen customs. Some new Christians continued their egg decorating and their homage to the pagan "Easter bunny." Over centuries, such traditions became cemented in what is today known as Christianity. These Easter customs were well established by the time the Scriptures were translated into English.

In recent years, many regular churchgoers have been questioning Easter and its ties to the ancient religions condemned by the Bible. Even the *Tonight Show* host Jay Leno discussed his heartfelt confusion as to what bunny rabbits and colorful eggs had to do with the resurrection of Jesus Christ. But now, for those who bother to examine the pages of their own Bible for themselves, the answer is clear: absolutely nothing.

CHAPTER FOUR

"GOD THE FATHER" IS NOT IN THE OLD TESTAMENT

DID YOU KNOW baby Jesus was a demolition expert before He soiled His first diaper? He was a master stone engraver before His first hiccup. He was also an inventor, tour guide, and champion wrestler. Baby Jesus was all these things and many more—even before He spent His first five minutes in a Bethlehem manger.

It sounds unbelievable, but like the U.S. Army motto, "We do more before 9 a.m. than most people do all day," Jesus did more than any man or woman could do in an entire life span before He was wrapped in swaddling clothes some two thousand years ago.

Perhaps this chapter will surprise even longtime churchgoers who never put the pieces together to see the whole picture of Jesus' life, especially the early years. I mean, the *really* early years. Not the years of His childhood on Earth. I mean the years before He was born as a baby to Joseph and Mary. Baby Jesus was alive long before showing up in the manger, and He certainly was no baby.

According to the Bible, the Jesus of the New Testament had an extensive history before He was born as a human being. He had numerous "guest appearances" in the Old Testament, often doing the unexpected. Among His exploits: firebombing a city to demolish it (Genesis 19:24), using His own finger to etch His handwriting into stone (Exodus 32:16), wrestling with His loved ones (Genesis 32:24), and designing and creating the universe (John 1:3).

Those learning this for the first time may be blown away by the information that's coming. It's different from what most people think or teach. But we'll take our time and ease into it, so it becomes clear who this baby Jesus really is.

What's in a Name?

To explore the long résumé of Jesus, start by looking at the New Testament. Among these twenty-seven books, Jesus is known by a variety of names and titles. For instance, He is:

The Word (John 1:1, 14; Revelation 19:13)

The Saviour (Luke 2:11; Philippians 3:20; Titus 2:13)

The Son of God (Luke 1:35; Matthew 8:29; John 1:34)

The Son of man (Matthew 13:41; 16:27; Luke 24:7)

The first and the last (Revelation 1:11, 17; 22:13)

King of kings (1 Timothy 6:15; Revelation 17:14; 19:16)

Lord of lords (1 Timothy 6:15; Revelation 17:14; 19:16)

The gospel of John wastes no time providing Jesus' true identity. John, who calls Jesus "the Word," says Jesus is God Himself, the Creator of all things: "In the beginning was the Word, and the Word was with God, and the Word was God. The same was in the beginning with God. All things were made by him; and without him was not any thing made that was made" (1:1–3).

The New Living Translation emphasizes the fact that Jesus was not making His debut in the manger, but has been alive forever: "In the beginning the Word already existed. He was with God, and he was God" (v.1).

This person Jesus, whom John calls "the Word," was apparently alive with God the Father at the very beginning. Not only that, but He also *was* God. John says it was "the Word" who created everything and who eventually left His place with God the Father to become a human being.

And the Word was made flesh, and dwelt among us, (and we beheld his glory, the glory as of the only begotten of the Father,) full of grace and truth . . . He was in the world, and the world was made by him, and the world knew him not. He came unto his own, and his own received him not. But as many as received him, to them gave he power to become the sons of God, even to them that believe in his name. (1:14, 10–12)

The scenario is reminiscent of the 1995 song "One of Us" by Joan Osborne, in which she asks, "What if God was one of us?" The gospel of John has the answer, pointing out that God already was one of us. Long after He had created it all, Jesus lived, breathed, ate, worked, sweated, preached, and died here on planet Earth.

This first chapter of John is the key to understanding the entire Bible. And what it points to is that Jesus Christ is the God of the Old Testament. Write that down somewhere and memorize it.

Jesus Christ is the God of the Old Testament. His appearance in a manger in Bethlehem two thousand years ago was not His beginning. His existence did not commence in the womb of His human mother, Mary. Jesus Christ was alive a long time prior to that. He, along with God the Father, was in existence forever, not as a human being, but as a member of the very Family of God.

I have spoken with countless individuals who are under the mistaken impression that the God of the Old Testament is a mean, harsh "God the Father," and things changed for the better when He sent His Son, Jesus, into the world during New Testament times. This is not the case. Jesus Christ also interacted with humans in Old Testament times.

Where's Dad?

If you search the Bible, the phrases "God the Father" and "God our Father" do not appear anywhere in the Old Testament! It's true. Not once. Zero. Zilch. Nada. Squatta. They are just not there. Feel free to go ahead and read the entire Old Testament right now to be sure. I'll patiently await your return.

Amazingly, while those titles are absent in the Old Testament, they seem to be everywhere in the New Testament, where "God the Father" can be found a dozen times, and "God our Father" is in eleven verses. For example:

And that every tongue should confess that Jesus Christ is Lord, to the glory of God the Father. (Philippians 2:11)

Grace unto you, and peace, from God our Father and the Lord Jesus Christ. (2 Thessalonians 1:2)

Paul, an apostle, (not of men, neither by man, but by Jesus Christ, and God the Father, who raised him from the dead;) (Galatians 1:1)

As I pointed out earlier, John's gospel indicates Jesus is the Creator of all things and that "without him was not any thing made that was made."

Paul reiterated that everything came into existence because Jesus created it: "For by him were all things created, that are in heaven, and that are in earth, visible and invisible, whether they be thrones, or dominions, or principalities, or powers: all things were created by him, and for him" (Colossians 1:16).

The book of Genesis makes statements such as these:

In the beginning God created the heaven and the earth. (1:1)

And God said, Let there be light: and there was light. (1:3)

And God made the beast of the earth after his kind, and cattle after their kind, and every thing that creepeth upon the earth after his kind: and God saw that it was good. (1:25)

So God created man in his own image, in the image of God created he him; male and female created he them. (1:27)

Substitute the name Jesus for the word *God* in each of these verses, and it becomes clear that Jesus was the Creator of the world, as John revealed in the opening to his gospel.

Holy Moses Was Wholly About Jesus

It is not only a few isolated verses that support this concept of Jesus being the God of the Old Testament. John noted that Jesus told the Jews who were persecuting Him that the Old Testament writings of Moses were mainly about Him—Jesus.

Search the scriptures; for in them ye think ye have eternal life: and they are they which testify of me. (John 5:39)

For had ye believed Moses, ye would have believed me: for he wrote of me. (John 5:46)

Notice, Jesus was saying that Moses wrote and testified about *Him*. He did not mention God the Father.

Furthermore, John went out of his way to make a distinction between Jesus and God the Father, stressing that no human being has ever even seen God the Father or heard His voice at any time:

No one has ever seen God. But his only Son, who is himself God, is near to the Father's heart; he has told us about him. (John 1:18 NLT)

And the Father himself, which hath sent me, hath borne witness of me. Ye have neither heard his voice at any time, nor seen his shape. (John 5:37)

No man hath seen God at any time. (1 John 4:12)

This is the core of the matter. According to the Bible, God was seen and heard many times in the Old Testament. He appeared in person to Abraham, Isaac, and Jacob, and even talked with Moses face-to-face. But if Jesus is correct that no one has ever seen God at any time, neither hearing His voice nor seeing His shape, then who was it that everyone in the Old Testament saw and heard? It was Jesus Christ in His life before being born as a human!

Believe it or not, the Bible does not say "God the Father" created all things. It does not say "God our Father" destroyed Sodom and Gomorrah. Nowhere does it say "God the Father" spoke to the patriarchs or the prophets. It does not say "God our Father" led the Israelites out of Egypt and on a forty-year tour through the wilderness. "God the Father" did not wrestle with Jacob. It is the God who later came to be known as Jesus who did all these things.

Somehow, many people have understood it backward. They assume "God the Father" is the God of the Old Testament, and that Jesus is the God of the New Testament. But it's the other way around. Jesus is the God of the Old Testament, and God the Father, though He existed eternally with Jesus, was finally revealed and explained by Jesus in the New! Stunning, isn't it?

Here is more proof to demonstrate that Jesus is the God of the Old Testament. What did the God of the Old Testament say would be His name for all eternity? Did He ask to be called "Father"? No.

> And Moses said unto God, Behold, when I come unto the children of Israel, and shall say unto them, The God of your fathers hath sent me unto you; and they shall say to me, What is his name? what shall I say unto them? And God said unto Moses, I AM THAT I AM: and he said, Thus shalt thou say unto the children of Israel, I AM hath sent me unto you. And God said moreover unto Moses, Thus shalt thou say unto the children of Israel, The LORD God of your fathers, the God of Abraham, the God of Isaac, and the God of Jacob, hath sent me unto you: this is my name for ever, and this is my memorial unto all generations. (Exodus 3:13–15)

There you have it. The God of the Old Testament is not named "Father." He is "I AM THAT I AM," or more simply "I AM."

Over the centuries, there has been a lot of discussion about the true meaning of this name of God, the "I AM." Scholars have suggested alternatives such as "I will be what I will be." In today's modern language, here are some additional phrases to help you grasp the significance of God's name:

I am what it's all about.

I am the be all and end-all.

I am the ever-existent one.

I'm da bomb.

Jesus Christ: I AM

While the God of the Old Testament said "I AM" would be His name forever, Jesus was nearly stoned by the Jews for calling Himself by the same name. He called Himself "I AM," no less, when He was explaining to them that He had personally met the patriarch Abraham thousands of years earlier. John's gospel records the questions from Jesus' fellow Jews: "Art thou greater than our father Abraham, which is dead? and the prophets are dead: whom makest thou thyself?" (8:53).

Jesus responded in verse 56, "Your father Abraham rejoiced to see my day: and he saw it, and was glad."

And the key question and nearly deadly answer:

Then said the Jews unto him, Thou art not yet fifty years old, and hast thou seen Abraham?

Jesus said unto them, Verily, verily, I say unto you, Before Abraham was, I am.

Then took they up stones to cast at him: but Jesus hid himself, and went out of the temple, going through the midst of them, and so passed by. (John 8:57–59)

The Jews knew exactly what Jesus meant. He had a relationship with Abraham and publicly identified Himself as the "I AM" of the Old Testament, the same one who spoke to Moses. Thus, they sought to stone Him for calling Himself God, the God of the Old Testament.

It's strange how the Jews who hated Jesus during His earthly ministry were able to understand this truth, and yet so many Christians today who say they "love the Lord" have no idea Jesus clearly identified Himself as the God of the Old Testament.

The Old and the New

As mentioned before, Jesus is known by other names and titles in the New Testament. Given that Jesus is the God of the Old Testament, those same titles found in the Old Testament are stunning. Here are a few examples.

Jesus as the savior and redeemer in the Old Testament:

I, even I, am the LORD; and beside me there is no saviour. (Isaiah 43:11)

Verily thou art a God that hidest thyself, O God of Israel, the Saviour. (Isaiah 45:15)

All flesh shall know that I the LORD am thy Saviour and thy Redeemer, the mighty One of Jacob. (Isaiah 49:26)

Yet I am the LORD thy God from the land of Egypt, and thou shalt know no god but me: for there is no saviour beside me. (Hosea 13:4)

The New Testament makes it clear Jesus is the savior of mankind:

For unto you is born this day in the city of David a Saviour, which is Christ the Lord. (Luke 2:11)

For our conversation is in heaven; from whence also we look for the Saviour, the Lord Jesus Christ. (Philippians 3.20)

And we have seen and do testify that the Father sent the Son to be the Saviour of the world. (1 John 4:14)

Jesus as "the first and the last" in the Old Testament:

Thus saith the LORD the King of Israel, and his redeemer the LORD of hosts; I am the first, and I am the last; and beside me there is no God. (Isaiah 44:6)

Hearken unto me, O Jacob and Israel, my called; I am he; I am the first, I also am the last. (Isaiah 48:12)

Jesus as "the first and the last" in the New Testament:

Fear not; I am the first and the last: I am he that liveth, and was dead; and, behold, I am alive for evermore. (Revelation 1:17–18)

I am Alpha and Omega, the beginning and the end, the first and the last. (Revelation 22:13)

Jesus is also called "the Rock" throughout Scripture. The Old Testament states, "Because I will publish the name of the LORD: ascribe ye greatness unto our God. He is the Rock, his work is perfect: for all his ways are judgment: a God of truth and without iniquity, just and right is he" (Deuteronomy 32:3–4).

The New Testament uses that same capitalized word *Rock* to identify Jesus—not God the Father—as the one leading Moses and the Israelites out of Egypt and through the wilderness in Old Testament times: "And did all drink the same spiritual drink: for they drank of that spiritual Rock that followed them: and that Rock was Christ" (1 Corinthians 10:4).

That Rock was Christ. Smacks you right across the face, doesn't it? Go ahead, highlight the words in your own Bible.

By now, it's clear that Jesus Christ is the God of the Old Testament. He even made a few guest appearances before He became Mary's newborn. Remember, Jesus Himself said that no human being has ever seen God the Father.

No man hath seen God at any time; the only begotten Son, which is in the bosom of the Father, he hath declared him. (John 1:18)

And the Father himself, which hath sent me, hath borne witness of me. Ye have neither heard his voice at any time, nor seen his shape. (John 5:37)

And, as John corroborates,

No man hath seen God at any time. (1 John 4:12)

Part of Jesus' mission when he lived as a human was to declare, or reveal for the first time, God the Father. So all of the following instances of God or the "LORD" involve Jesus Christ in His prehuman life.

There is an incredible selection from which to choose, since virtually the entire Old Testament is devoted to Jesus. But let's examine some of the most dazzling episodes.

Power Lunch

I mentioned previously that Jesus was a demolition expert before He soiled His first diaper, and that Jesus met Abraham. Both claims are true and are found in the eighteenth and nineteenth chapters of Genesis. The Scripture indicates that the Lord—Jesus, not God the Father—appeared in the form of man. He also had two angels with Him. Jesus sat down for a meal with Abraham and bargained about the fate of Sodom and Gomorrah, before personally demolishing the cities by fire and brimstone.

And the LORD appeared unto him in the plains of Mamre: and he sat in the tent door in the heat of the day; and he lift up his eyes and looked, and, lo, three men stood by him: and when he saw them, he ran to meet them from the tent door, and bowed himself toward the ground, and said, My LORD, if now I have found favour in thy sight, pass not away, I pray thee, from thy servant: Let a little water, I pray you, be fetched, and wash your feet, and rest yourselves under the tree: And I will fetch a morsel of bread, and comfort ye your hearts; after that ye shall pass on: for therefore are ye come to your servant. And they said, So do, as thou hast said. (18.1–5)

This was not some vision or dream at night. It was taking place "in the heat of the day," probably around noon or early afternoon. Abraham saw what appeared to be men and immediately ran to them; he then bowed toward the ground. It's obvious Abraham recognized who had arrived, since he addressed Him as "my Lord." Abraham saw God Himself. Jesus appeared as a man, and Abraham asked to wash His feet and get Him some food while He rested under a tree.

For those who may not have read the Bible before, Abraham was able to recognize Jesus easily, since this was not the first time the Lord (Jesus) had appeared to him. In earlier chapters, we read:

And the LORD appeared unto Abram, and said, Unto thy seed will I give this land: and there builded he an altar unto the LORD, who appeared unto him. (12:7)

And when Abram was ninety years old and nine, the LORD appeared to Abram, and said unto him, I am the Almighty God; walk before me, and be thou perfect. And I will make my covenant between me and thee, and will multiply thee exceedingly. And Abram fell on his face: and God talked with him, saying, As for me, behold, my covenant is with thee, and thou shalt be a father of many nations. Neither shall thy name any more be called Abram, but thy name shall be Abraham; for a father of many nations have I made thee. (17:1–5)

At least two other people besides Abraham, God, and the two angels were present at the lunch meeting. These witnesses even participated in the action and conversation. One was Abraham's wife, Sarah, and the other was a young servant who helped prepare the food for the meal.

And Abraham hastened into the tent unto Sarah, and said, Make ready quickly three measures of fine meal, knead it, and make cakes upon the hearth. And Abraham ran unto the herd, and fetcht a calf tender and good, and gave it unto a young man; and he hasted to dress it. And he took butter, and milk, and the calf which he had dressed, and set it before them; and he stood by them under the tree, and they did eat. (18:6–8)

Once lunch was over, Jesus and the two angels got up to head toward Sodom. Abraham walked them on their way and tried to persuade Jesus not to destroy Sodom if some righteous inhabitants were living there.

And the men rose up from thence, and looked toward Sodom: and Abraham went with them to bring them on the way. And the LORD said, Shall I hide from Abraham that thing which I do; seeing that Abraham shall surely become a great and mighty nation, and all the nations of the earth shall be blessed in him? (vv. 16–18)

Note that God also uses personal pronouns "I" and "me" when discussing His mission.

And the LORD said, Because the cry of Sodom and Gomorrah is great, and because their sin is very grievous; I will go down now, and see whether they have done altogether according to the cry of it, which is come unto me; and if not, I will know. And the men turned their faces from thence, and went toward Sodom: but Abraham stood yet before the LORD. (vv. 20–22)

I hate to sound repetitive, but remember, no one has seen God the Father at any time. Jesus Himself said so: "Ye have neither heard his voice at any time, nor seen his shape" (John 5:37).

So Abraham had a very real, personal discussion with the person who would later be known as Jesus Christ. He did not see or talk to God the Father, since no human being ever has. And during this meeting, Abraham even called Jesus "the Judge of all the earth," a title most Christians would have no problem attaching to Jesus (2 Timothy 4:1).

And Abraham drew near, and said, Wilt thou also destroy the righteous with the wicked? Peradventure there be fifty righteous within the city:

wilt thou also destroy and not spare the place for the fifty righteous that are therein? That be far from thee to do after this manner, to slay the righteous with the wicked: and that the righteous should be as the wicked, that be far from thee: Shall not the Judge of all the earth do right? (Genesis 18:23–25)

The climax of the story came when Jesus destroyed the sinful cities: "Then the LORD rained upon Sodom and upon Gomorrah brimstone and fire from the LORD out of heaven; and he overthrew those cities, and all the plain, and all the inhabitants of the cities, and that which grew upon the ground" (19:24–25).

Holy Smackdown

Another guest appearance by Jesus in the Old Testament was when He wrestled Abraham's grandson Jacob throughout the night. It was a real wrestling match, long before wrestling became phony.

Genesis records the celebrity match-up between God (Jesus) and Jacob. At the end of this "WrestleMania," God changed Jacob's name to Israel. It happened as Jacob was preparing to meet his brother, Esau, after many years of separation: "And Jacob was left alone; and there wrestled a man with him until the breaking of the day. And when he saw that he prevailed not against him, he touched the hollow of his thigh; and the hollow of Jacob's thigh was out of joint, as he wrestled with him" (32:24–25).

As the scene unfolds, Jacob is wrestling with an unidentified man, and apparently the wrestling went on for some time, "until the breaking of the day." Both participants were physically adept, and the match was extremely close, prompting the mystery man to touch part of Jacob's thigh and put it out of joint. Even then, Jacob kept his partner in some kind of iron-grip lock, prompting the unknown wrestler to ask to be freed. Jacob, however, realized the man's true identity: "Then the man said, 'Let me go, for it is dawn.' But Jacob panted, 'I will not let you go unless you bless me'" (v. 26 NLT).

After having his thigh thrown out of joint, Jacob asked for this man's blessing, giving the second clue that this is no ordinary man with whom Jacob is dealing, but someone superior to himself:

"What is your name?" the man asked.

He replied, "Jacob."

"Your name will no longer be Jacob," the man told him.

"It is now Israel, because you have struggled with both God and men and have won." (vv. 27–28 NLT)

This quote could be taken two ways. One is that the mystery wrestler informed Jacob that he (Jacob) had been struggling throughout life and had now prevailed. But the second and more likely option is that God was revealing Himself to Jacob, telling him he had just struggled (wrestled) with God and had prevailed. Not only that, but this mystery wrestler, who apparently had the power to zap joints out of alignment and give blessings, also had the authority to change someone's name!

The clincher that this was indeed God becomes even clearer as the story continues.

"What is your name?" Jacob asked him.

"Why do you ask?" the man replied. Then he blessed Jacob there.

(v. 29 NLT)

While we are never really told why, there is a motif throughout the Bible of people asking God for His name. He sometimes responded by wondering why they wanted to know it, as if it did not matter.

At that point in time, Jacob—along with his father, Isaac, and grandfather, Abraham—had not been provided a specific, personal name for God, so it's no wonder his curiosity was piqued. God did not reveal His personal name until Moses came along in Exodus. While the unknown wrestler found it interesting that Jacob sought to know his identity, all we know is that the man blessed Jacob and changed his name to Israel, not whether He answered Jacob's question.

The precise identity of the man, who in reality is Jesus, is confirmed in the next verse, when Jacob gave a name to the venue where he had this incredible experience: "Jacob named the place Peniel—'face of God'—for he said, 'I have seen God face to face, yet my life has been spared'" (v. 30 NLT).

There is no way around it. Jacob saw God face-to-face and named the location "face of God" in honor of seeing (and wrestling) God in person. In addition, there is no explanatory note suggesting Jacob was mistaken in believing he had seen the face of God.

For more evidence that this was a real event and not a dream or vision, the Bible points out that Jacob left the arena with an obvious limp: "The sun rose as he left Peniel, and he was limping because of his hip. That is why even today the people of Israel don't eat meat from near the hip, in memory of what happened that night" (vv. 31–32 NLT).

Even in today's culture, this event is the single reason leg of lamb is usually not for sale in a kosher food store.

Jacob's wrestling match with God is recalled in the book of Hosea. The Old Testament prophet does not refer to Jacob's wrestling partner as a human but rather as a supernatural being: "Yes, he wrestled with the angel and won. He wept and pleaded for a blessing from him. There at Bethel he met God face to face, and God spoke to him" (12:4 NLT).

That same term, *angel*, is found when Jesus appeared to Moses for the first time: "And the angel of the LORD appeared unto him in a flame of fire out of the midst of a bush . . . Moreover he said, I am the God of thy father, the God of Abraham, the God of Isaac, and the God of Jacob. And Moses hid his face; for he was afraid to look upon God" (Exodus 3:2, 6).

It's quite evident this "angel of the LORD," "the God of Abraham, the God of Isaac, and the God of Jacob," was none other than Jesus Christ. People in the Old Testament never saw or heard "God the Father." The people saw Jesus. They talked to Him. They heard His voice. They bargained with Him. And one man even wrestled with Him.

Jesus is the same God who ordered light to shine from the very beginning, the same God who flooded the earth in Noah's day, and the same God who used His finger to write the Ten Commandments in stone tablets. He is the same God who begged and pleaded with His people to turn back to His instructions, and the same God who left His home in heaven to live and die just like everyone else.

The Old Testament is not about some grouchy old "God the Father." It's about Jesus. For those who think Jesus is solely found in the pages of the New Testament, you're only seeing a fraction of the story. So the next time you read the Old Testament, look carefully for Jesus Christ. You'll find Him on virtually every page.

CHAPTER FIVE

DAYS OF THE LIVING DEAD

JESUS CHRIST rose from the dead. This you already know from the Bible.

But did you know Jesus was not the only one who was resurrected? According to the Bible, many people were brought back to life. From the Old Testament to the New, deceased people of all ages were made alive again without acting like zombies. Their stories raise provocative questions about what happens to people once they die.

I See Dead People

The first instance of someone being "quickened"—that is to say, brought to life from the dead—is found in a brief story in the seventeenth chapter of 1 Kings. Elijah the prophet revived the son of a widow with whom he was staying:

> Some time later, the woman's son became sick. He grew worse and worse, and finally he died. She then said to Elijah, "O man of God, what have you done to me? Have you come here to punish my sins by killing my son?" But Elijah replied, "Give me your son." And he took the boy's body from her, carried him up to the upper room, where he lived, and laid the body on his bed. Then Elijah cried out to the LORD, "O LORD my God, why have you brought tragedy on this widow who has opened her home

to me, causing her son to die?" And he stretched himself out over the child three times and cried out to the LORD, "O LORD my God, please let this child's life return to him." The LORD heard Elijah's prayer, and the life of the child returned, and he came back to life! Then Elijah brought him down from the upper room and gave him to his mother. "Look, your son is alive!" he said. Then the woman told Elijah, "Now I know for sure that you are a man of God, and that the LORD truly speaks through you." (vv. 17–24 NLT)

This first instance of a dead person being brought back from the grave was a physical resurrection. The boy who died and was revived was not given eternal life but restored to his normal, flesh-and-blood existence. Nonetheless, it's clearly significant that a person was able to have life infused into his corpse. The boy's mother was undoubtedly thankful, immediately recognizing the revival as an act of God and seeing Elijah as His legitimate representative.

Lifeboy No. 2

The second person resurrected was a boy who lived during the time of Elisha, the prophet who succeeded Elijah. The child was the son of a Shunammite woman who had been barren her entire life. When she showed Elisha kindness and hospitality, God granted her the blessing of having a child.

One day, while working in the fields, the boy complained of a severe headache: "And he said unto his father, My head, my head. And he said to a lad, Carry him to his mother. And when he had taken him, and brought him to his mother, he sat on her knees till noon, and then died" (2 Kings 4:19–20).

Elisha's servant tried unsuccessfully to remedy the situation, but Elisha himself had better results.

And when Elisha was come into the house, behold, the child was dead, and laid upon his bed. He went in therefore, and shut the door upon them twain, and prayed unto the LORD. And he went up, and lay upon the child, and put his mouth upon his mouth, and his eyes upon his eyes, and his hands upon his hands: and stretched himself upon the child; and the flesh of the child waxed warm. Then he returned, and walked in the house to and fro; and went up, and stretched himself upon him: and the child sneezed seven times, and the child opened his eyes. (vv. 32–35)

Again, this was a resurrection to physical, temporal, mortal life rather than eternal life. Before Elisha got involved, the dead child's body was already cold. The text notes that once Elisha began to help, the boy's body started to heat up again. After Elisha had lain on the body one final time, the boy started sneezing and awoke from death.

1 Dead Guy + 1 Dead Guy = 1 Dead Guy Alive

The third example of a resurrection in the Old Testament is quite bizarre. It actually involved two dead people, one of whom jumped back to life as soon as he came in contact with the other. The two-verse account in 2 Kings again concerns the prophet Elisha, who was already dead and in the grave.

> Then Elisha died and was buried. Groups of Moabite raiders used to invade the land each spring. Once when some Israelites were burying a man, they spied a band of these raiders. So they hastily threw the body they were burying into the tomb of Elisha. But as soon as the body touched Elisha's bones, the dead man revived and jumped to his feet! (13:20–21 NLT)

There it is. No bones about it. The dead man, having touched the long-decayed remains of Elisha, suddenly sprang back to life and jumped to his feet! The people laying their friend to rest must have been astonished to see him instantly rejoin the living, especially with no visible act of intervention.

During the course of his lifetime, Elisha had been noted for performing numerous miracles, and it appears he was so full of the power of God that even long after his death, the remnants of this prophet were able to bring a fellow Israelite back from the dead.

New Testament Resurrections

Resurrections in the Bible are not just an Old Testament phenomenon; many people in the New had their lives restored to them as well.

One New Testament story recounts how Jesus resurrected a widow's son who was being carried for burial: "Then he walked over to the coffin and touched it, and the bearers stopped. 'Young man,' he said, 'get up.' Then the dead boy sat up and began to talk to those around him! And Jesus gave him back to his mother" (Luke 7:14–15 NLT).

Another case involves a local ruler who asked Jesus to lay His hand upon his dead twelve-year-old daughter so she would live again:

> There came from the ruler of the synagogue's house certain which said, Thy daughter is dead: why troublest thou the Master any further? As soon as Jesus heard the word that was spoken, he saith unto the ruler of the synagogue, Be not afraid, only believe . . . And he cometh to the house of the ruler of the synagogue, and seeth the tumult, and them that wept and wailed greatly. And when he was come in, he saith unto them, Why make ye this ado, and weep? The damsel is not dead, but sleepeth. And they laughed him to scorn. But when he had put them all out, he taketh the father and the mother of the damsel, and them that were with him, and entereth in where the damsel was lying. And he took the damsel by the hand, and said unto her, Talitha cumi; which is, being interpreted, Damsel, I say unto thee, arise. And straightway the damsel arose, and walked; for she was of the age of twelve years. And they were astonished with a great astonishment. (Mark 5:35–42)

It's interesting to note Jesus' comment about the girl not being dead but asleep. The Bible often refers to death as sleep, but it also shows that it's not the typical sleep from which people awake every day. In cases like this, it takes the miraculous power of God to awaken the dead.

The sleeping analogy was also used in the famous story of Lazarus, the personal friend of Jesus who died and remained dead for several days before being brought back to life. As shown in the gospel of John, Lazarus was not simply sleeping, near death, in a coma, or pretending to be dead.

> Our friend Lazarus sleepeth; but I go, that I may awake him out of sleep. Then said his disciples, Lord, if he sleeps, he shall do well. Howbeit Jesus spake of his death: but they thought that he had spoken of taking of rest in sleep. Then said Jesus unto them plainly, Lazarus is dead. (11:11–14)

The text went the extra mile to explain that Lazarus had been in a tomb for four days. It's clear that everyone around knew he was dead, as they all expected the horrific odor of death when the tomb was opened: "When Jesus came, he found that he had lain in the grave four days already . . . Jesus said, Take ye away the stone. Martha, the sister of him that was dead, saith unto him, Lord, by this time he stinketh: for he hath been dead four days" (vv. 17, 39).

Despite the warning about how rank the stench would be, Jesus spoke directly to His dead friend, ordering him to arise and emerge from the tomb.

And when he thus had spoken, he cried with a loud voice, Lazarus, come forth. And he that was dead came forth, bound hand and foot with graveclothes: and his face was bound about with a napkin. Jesus saith unto them, Loose him, and let him go. Then many of the Jews which came to Mary, and had seen the things which Jesus did, believed on him. (vv. 43–45)

After four days of death and decay, some one hundred hours of ripening in the grave, Lazarus was instantly brought back to life by the command of Jesus.

Dead Men Walking

Of course, the most famous resurrection from the dead is that of Jesus Christ Himself. But what shocks many is that a large number of His followers were brought back to life as Jesus was killed! Not only that, they strolled into downtown Jerusalem to appear to other people!

The underreported passage is found in the gospel of Matthew.

Jesus, when he had cried again with a loud voice, yielded up the ghost. And, behold, the veil of the temple was rent in twain from the top to the bottom; and the earth did quake, and the rocks rent; and the graves were opened; and many bodies of the saints which slept arose, and came out of the graves after his resurrection, and went into the holy city, and appeared unto many. (27:50–53)

The passage dazzled me to such an extent that I had to check other translations to be sure of what was really taking place here. The New International Version puts it simply: "The tombs broke open and the bodies of many holy people who had died were raised to life. They came out of the tombs, and after Jesus' resurrection they went into the holy city and appeared to many people" (vv. 52–53).

The New Living Translation translates it like this, along with a footnote:

> At that moment the curtain in the Temple was torn in two, from top to bottom. The earth shook, rocks split apart, and tombs opened. The bodies of many godly men and women who had died were raised from the dead after Jesus' resurrection. They left the cemetery, went into the holy city of Jerusalem, and appeared to many people. (vv. 51–53)

Its footnoted version has it this way: "The earth shook, rocks split apart, tombs opened, and the bodies of many godly men and women who had died were raised from the dead. After Jesus' resurrection, they left the cemetery, went into the holy city of Jerusalem, and appeared to many people."

There is consensus among Bible translations that dead followers of Jesus came back to life and proceeded out of their tombs at the time of Jesus' own resurrection from the grave. Their tombs were opened, and these newly "undead" people made their way not to heaven but to Jerusalem to show others they were no longer six feet under.

It sounds like something out of a zombie flick, except these were not typical staggering, moaning zombies looking to devour human flesh.

If such an event were to happen today, every network would have breaking news alerts instantly. The *Today Show* might even break away from its cooking segment to report such an incredible event. At least we can hope it would.

This would be one of the biggest news stories of all time, and everyone would want a piece of it.

Some Bible readers do not believe dead people actually came back to life in the gospel account. Instead, they suggest an alternate theory. They speculate that random graves were opened by an earthquake, and corpses spilled out.

Yet there are some problems with such a scenario. First, the Scripture says, "Many bodies of the saints which slept arose, and came out of the graves after his resurrection, and went into the holy city" (v. 52–53).

The key words in the passage are *arose* and *went*. It does not say they tumbled or floated there, or were tossed on a cart and wheeled into the city. Arising and going implies a return to a living state, whereby they could transport themselves to their destination. Jesus Himself had said, "I am the resurrection, and the life: he that believeth in me, though he were dead, yet shall he live" (John 11:25).

Plus, as we've seen, the Bible previously documented other dead people being raised to flesh-and-blood life.

But even more problematic for this theory is the fact that Scripture specifies "many bodies of the saints which slept" arose. Read that phrase again: *Many bodies of the saints which slept.* These were human beings who were obedient to God during their lifetimes. The Bible does not say others—including sinners—in the general population arose and went into the holy city—only the followers of God.

If these bodies came out of the tombs as a result of the earthquake, then we should expect the text to reflect that by generically stating something to the effect of "many dead bodies." Yet it went out of its way to explicitly state that it was people of the true faith who arose. Hence, they were indeed raised back to life.

Power Surge

It was not just Jesus, though, who had the power to raise people from the dead. The New Testament indicates that His apostles also had that power.

One instance recorded in Acts involved a believer named Tabitha who became sick and died:

> But Peter put them all forth, and kneeled down, and prayed; and turning him to the body said, Tabitha, arise. And she opened her eyes: and when she saw Peter, she sat up. And he gave her his hand, and lifted her up, and when he had called the saints and widows, presented her alive. (9:40–41)

Such an account should come as little surprise to frequent Bible readers, as Jesus Himself instructed His followers to bring back people from the grave: "Heal the sick, cleanse the lepers, raise the dead, cast out devils: freely ye have received, freely give" (Matthew 10:8).

This resurrection, along with all the others, raises important questions. Were these dead people alive in heaven right after they died? After all, many churches teach that when God's people die, they immediately go to heaven. Surprisingly, there is no verse in the Bible that specifically indicates that, though many people share that belief.

The Bible does not record what the resurrected individuals experienced, if anything, once they had died. Not a peep about how awesome it was to be on the so-called "other side." No astounding tales of harp concerts, sky surfing, or cloud hockey. Even if they were with God in that "better place" often mentioned at funerals, is it possible they would not be thrilled to be suddenly yanked from the very presence of God and thrown back into their frail, human bodies?

I certainly wouldn't.

CHAPTER SIX

IMAGINE THERE'S THREE HEAVENS

IF YOU HAVE not been shocked yet, then sit down, buckle up, and make sure your seat is pushed all the way to the upright position. You are about to take off into the heavens, and by the time you land, you will find out what the Bible *really* says about heaven itself. You'll discover that there's more than one place called heaven, and you may even come to a new conclusion about whether or not good people go to heaven immediately when they die.

Most people are probably familiar with the famous song "Imagine" by John Lennon. The song features the well-known opening lyric, "Imagine there's no heaven." However, I'd like to suggest a new line: "Imagine there's *three* heavens."

In fact, according to Scripture, no imagination is necessary regarding the number of heavens. The Bible speaks of not one, not two, but three distinct places that all go by the name of "heaven." Yet most people remain ignorant of this reality because it is rarely mentioned in church.

On what grounds can I claim there are three heavens? The apostle Paul said so, making specific mention of "the third heaven" in one of his letters. It does not take a rocket scientist to realize there cannot be a third heaven unless a first and second heaven also exist. We'll examine that third heaven momentarily, but we must first take a look at the first and second types so the differences are clear.

The First Heaven

The first type of heaven is the sky. It is the air. It's the atmosphere of planet Earth. It's where the winds blow, where clouds gather, and the place from which birds take target practice on your car's new paint job. One could easily substitute the word *sky* for heaven or heavens in the following verses:

> Sing unto the LORD with thanksgiving; sing praise upon the harp unto our God: who covereth the heaven with clouds, who prepareth rain for the earth, who maketh grass to grow upon the mountains. (Psalm 147:7–8)

> Look unto the heavens, and see; and behold the clouds which are higher than thou. (Job 35:5)

> I will even give them into the hand of their enemies, and into the hand of them that seek their life: and their dead bodies shall be for meat unto the fowls of the heaven, and to the beasts of the earth. (Jeremiah 34:20)

When the Tower of Babel was being built, the goal was to build it to the "heavens": "Then they said, 'Come, let us build ourselves a city, with a tower that reaches to the heavens'" (Genesis 11:4 NIV).

The New Living Translation doesn't even use the word *heavens* but instead reads, "Let's build a great city with a tower that reaches to the *skies*" (emphasis added).

The Second Heaven

The second type of heaven is outer space, the home of the stars and planets:

> When I consider thy heavens, the work of thy fingers, the moon and the stars, which thou hast ordained . . . (Psalm 8:3)

> And I will make thy seed to multiply as the stars of heaven, and will give unto thy seed all these countries; and in thy seed shall all the nations of the earth be blessed. (Genesis 26:4)

> For the stars of heaven and the constellations thereof shall not give their light: the sun shall be darkened in his going forth, and the moon shall not cause her light to shine. (Isaiah 13:10)

The Third Heaven

The third heaven is not a strange concept. In fact, it's probably what most people think "heaven" is. The third heaven refers specifically to the throne and dwelling place of God. It's where God lives. Though the third heaven remains invisible to our human eyes, God and the angels exist and dwell in this unseen dimension.

Here is where Paul mentioned the third heaven:

I know a man in Christ who fourteen years ago was caught up to the third heaven. Whether it was in the body or out of the body I do not know—God knows. And I know that this man—whether in the body or apart from the body I do not know, but God knows—was caught up to paradise. He heard inexpressible things, things that man is not permitted to tell. (2 Corinthians 12:2–4 NIV)

Paul was discussing a tremendous vision he had about someone (probably himself) who was "caught up to the third heaven." He called this third heaven "paradise," and claimed that fantastic things were said—things so amazing, they could not be repeated.

Many different translations of the Bible consistently use "the third heaven." But there cannot be a third heaven unless there are also first and second heavens. Verses that indicate the third heaven as the dwelling place of God include:

Then hear thou their prayer and their supplication in heaven thy dwelling place, and maintain their cause. (1 Kings 8:49)

Then hear thou from heaven thy dwelling place, and forgive, and render unto every man according unto all his ways, whose heart thou knowest; (for thou only knowest the hearts of the children of men). (2 Chronicles 6:30)

Then hear thou from the heavens, even from thy dwelling place, their prayer and their supplications, and maintain their cause, and forgive thy people which have sinned against thee. (2 Chronicles 6:39)

And no man hath ascended up to heaven, but he that came down from heaven, even the Son of man which is in heaven. (John 3:13)

And the armies which were in heaven followed him upon white horses, clothed in fine linen, white and clean. (Revelation 19:14)

And another angel came out of the temple which is in heaven, he also having a sharp sickle. (Revelation 14:17)

This notion of the third heaven, however, will challenge what millions assume will happen after we die.

Heaven on Earth

Many people have engrained in their minds that when they die, they immediately go to heaven if they have accepted Jesus. While most take this for granted, no verse in the Bible says, "We go to heaven when we die." For that matter, the Bible does not even contain the phrase "immortal soul." According to Scripture, only God is immortal, as the New Testament refers to God "who alone is immortal and who lives in unapproachable light, whom no one has seen or can see" (1 Timothy 6:16 NIV).

In fact, much in the Bible suggests that when Christians die, they do not go to heaven—at least not immediately. As stunning as it sounds, Scripture has plenty to say about the state of the dead, indicating there are no thoughts of any kind:

For the living know that they shall die: but the dead know not any thing. (Ecclesiastes 9:5)

There is no work, nor device, nor knowledge, nor wisdom, in the grave, whither thou goest. (Ecclesiastes 9:10)

The dead praise not the LORD, neither any that go down into silence. (Psalm 115:17)

His breath goeth forth, he returneth to his earth; in that very day his thoughts perish. (Psalm 146:4)

The Bible continually refers to death as a profound sleep. In Psalm 13:3, King David spoke of "the sleep of death." Thirty-six times, Scripture mentions a dead man who "slept with his fathers," including David himself: "So David slept with his fathers, and was buried in the city of David" (1 Kings 2:10).

Recall how Jesus raised Lazarus from the grave, saying his friend was asleep: "Our friend Lazarus sleepeth; but I go, that I may awake him out of sleep" (John 11:11).

The prophet Daniel spoke about resurrections from the sleep of death, noting that "many of them that sleep in the dust of the earth shall awake, some to everlasting life, and some to shame and everlasting contempt" (Daniel 12:2).

And the New Testament refers to deceased believers as those who "sleep in Jesus" (1 Thessalonians 4:14).

But the sleep of death is not the ultimate end for people. There is still great news. Though the Bible does not state that people go to heaven right away, it does say that heaven—the dwelling place of God—will come here in the future!

God's throne will exist in plain sight, and God will dwell with mankind here on solid ground, granting eternal life to those faithful to Him. In a sense, people will eventually be alive forever in "heaven"—not because they died and were instantly whisked to some invisible place in the sky, but because "the third heaven," God's own dwelling place, will appear, and God will reside on Earth.

In Revelation, an angel revealed this concept to the apostle John:

> And I John saw the holy city, new Jerusalem, coming down from God out of heaven, prepared as a bride adorned for her husband. And I heard a great voice out of heaven saying, Behold, the tabernacle of God is with men, and he will dwell with them, and they shall be his people, and God himself shall be with them, and be their God. (21:2–3)

Notice this holy city, the "new Jerusalem," is "coming down from God out of heaven." In the future, God will no longer be invisible. He is finally going to dwell with His people in a city called "new Jerusalem." At some point in the future, heaven on Earth will be a reality.

The last two chapters of Revelation describe some of the wonderful conditions in this heaven on Earth.

> And God shall wipe away all tears from their eyes; and there shall be no

more death, neither sorrow, nor crying, neither shall there be any more pain: for the former things are passed away. (21:4)

And the city had no need of the sun, neither of the moon, to shine in it: for the glory of God did lighten it, and the Lamb is the light thereof. (21:23)

And the angel showed me a pure river with the water of life, clear as crystal, flowing from the throne of God and of the Lamb, coursing down the center of the main street. On each side of the river grew a tree of life, bearing twelve crops of fruit, with a fresh crop each month. The leaves were used for medicine to heal the nations. No longer will anything be cursed. For the throne of God and of the Lamb will be there, and his servants will worship him. (22:1–3 NLT)

There is a paradise with God still to come in the future. Heaven is actually coming here.

No One Has Gone to Heaven

Jesus Christ made a shocking statement about heaven—He indicated that no human has ever been there.

And no man hath ascended up to heaven, but he that came down from heaven, even the Son of man which is in heaven. (John 3:13)

No one has ever gone into heaven except the one who came from heaven—the Son of Man. (John 3:13 NIV)

Jesus said only He Himself had been to heaven, because He came from there. No one else has ever ascended to heaven! Even God's beloved King David did not immediately go to heaven when he died, or even after the resurrection of Jesus. The apostle Peter made note of that: "Men and brethren, let me freely speak unto you of the patriarch David, that he is both dead and buried, and his sepulchre is with us unto this day . . . For David is not ascended into the heavens" (Acts 2:29, 34).

However, Scripture indicates that David will someday be raised from the dead.

But they shall serve the LORD their God, and David their king, whom I will raise up unto them. (Jeremiah 30:9)

And David my servant shall be king over them; and they all shall have one shepherd: they shall also walk in my judgments, and observe my statutes, and do them. (Ezekiel 37:24)

There shall be weeping and gnashing of teeth, when ye shall see Abraham, and Isaac, and Jacob, and all the prophets, in the kingdom of God, and you yourselves thrust out. (Luke 13:28)

It seems obvious from these verses that David, Abraham, Isaac, Jacob, and all the prophets will be in the kingdom of God. The main question is: *when*?

Are We There Yet?

At many funerals, people seem to be under the impression that the person who died is already in heaven. You often hear comments such as: "The deceased is alive right now and in a much better place. He [or she] is looking down on us all at this moment, and smiling." It sounds comforting during a time of mourning, but the Bible actually suggests a *future* resurrection from the grave, one that does not take place until Jesus comes back to Earth, rather than an immediate ascent at the moment of death.

I know this concept is shocking, perhaps too jarring for some. But my point is that when people rely exclusively on all of the Bible without any preconceived notions and thousands of years of pagan-influenced doctrine, Scripture provides much more evidence for dead people being unaware of anything until Jesus' return than it does for an immediate trip to heaven. If some believe in an immortal soul or think they go to heaven when they die, that's fine. It doesn't offend me one bit. We'll all be with God in the end. But this subject is intriguing, to say the least, and is worth exploring.

When the first human being was created, we're told "God formed man of the dust of the ground, and breathed into his nostrils the breath of life; and man became a living soul" (Genesis 2:7).

Incidentally, the Hebrew word for soul, *nephesh*, is used in the Creation story not only for human beings but also for other creatures, from cattle to creeping things (1:24).

Not long after man was created, God told Adam he'd eventually be going back to the ground, since he was made up of dust and would return to dust. There's no mention of heaven in the text.

> In the sweat of thy face shalt thou eat bread, till thou return unto the ground: for out of it wast thou taken: for dust thou art, and unto dust shalt thou return. (3:19)

It was Satan the devil who subverted God's instructions and deceptively told Adam's wife: "Ye shall not surely die" (3:4). As stated before, Jesus said no one has gone to heaven except Himself (John 3:13). With that singular exception, no human biblical hero, including Abraham, has received the promise of eternal life yet: "These all died in faith, not having received the promises" (Hebrews 11:13). The phrases "immortal soul," "eternal soul," or "immortality of the soul" are not found anywhere in the Bible. However, we are told that only God has immortality (1 Timothy 6:16). Can souls actually die? Believe it or not, the Bible twice says yes, explaining that "the soul that sinneth, it shall die" (Ezekiel 18:4, 20).

In perhaps the single most famous verse in the Bible, Jesus said all people won't be alive forever. He spoke of two opposite destinies: perishing (complete destruction and death) or receiving eternal life:

> For God so loved the world, that he gave his only begotten Son, that whosoever believeth in him should not perish, but have everlasting life. (John 3:16)

And just to reiterate, people's thoughts perish the moment they die:

> For the living know that they shall die: but the dead know not any thing. (Ecclesiastes 9:5)

> His breath goeth forth, he returneth to his earth; in that very day his thoughts perish. (Psalm 146:4)

Having said all this, many are likely rushing to their Bibles to find some evidence that people are alive with God in heaven immediately when they die. Let's look at some of the most commonly cited quotes.

In Philippians 1:23, the apostle Paul talks about "having a desire to depart, and to be with Christ; which is far better."

Indeed, Paul referred to death and what comes after. It's obvious he really wanted to be with Christ. But notice, there's no mention of heaven! What's missing here is the answer to exactly *when* and *where* his being with Christ will take place.

In what are thought to be some of Paul's final words of his life, he stated:

> For I am now ready to be offered, and the time of my departure is at hand.
> I have fought a good fight, I have finished my course, I have kept the faith:
> Henceforth there is laid up for me a crown of righteousness, which the
> Lord, the righteous judge, shall give me at that day: and not to me only,
> but unto all them also that love his appearing. (2 Timothy 4:6–8)

Paul indicated he'll receive his reward "at that day." But is it the day of his death or another day? The final portion of the same sentence answers the issue, saying every other believer who loves Jesus' "appearing" will receive the reward at that same day.

Meanwhile, in 1 Thessalonians, Paul offered some words of comfort for believers, as he spoke of this appearing and the moment when people would rise out of their mortal slumber to finally be with Christ:

> According to the Lord's own word, we tell you that we who are still alive,
> who are left till the coming of the Lord, will certainly not precede those
> who have fallen asleep. For the Lord himself will come down from
> heaven, with a loud command, with the voice of the archangel and with
> the trumpet call of God, and the dead in Christ will rise first. After that,
> we who are still alive and are left will be caught up together with them
> in the clouds to meet the Lord in the air. And so we will be with the Lord
> forever. (4:15–17 NIV)

This is amazing information. Notice it does *not* say the "dead in Christ" are alive in heaven already. The text indicates they're asleep. They're dead! It is when the Lord comes down out of heaven when they're awakened. After that, all the other believers who were still alive on Earth will be suddenly caught up into the air with the freshly resurrected believers to meet Jesus who is entering the atmosphere as He descends out of His heavenly dwelling place. And that is when "we will be with the Lord forever." The event hasn't taken place yet, but Paul pinpointed the time when it will.

He said in 1 Corinthians: "For as in Adam all die, even so in Christ shall all be made alive. But every man in his own order: Christ the firstfruits; afterward they that are Christ's at his coming" (15:22–23).

Notice, the people who belong to Christ will be made alive "*at his coming.*"

Other translations make it clear:

But there is an order to this resurrection: Christ was raised first; then when Christ comes back, all his people will be raised. (v. 23 NLT)

But each in his own turn: Christ, the firstfruits; then, when he comes, those who belong to him. (NIV)

Paul made another interesting statement regarding life after death when he said he was "willing rather to be absent from the body, and to be present with the Lord" (2 Corinthians 5:8). Once again, there is no mention of heaven. The key question is exactly *when?*

The verse itself doesn't specify, but if we look just four verses before this statement, Paul noted "that mortality might be swallowed up of life" (v. 4).

Does this change from mortal to everlasting life occur immediately at the moment of death, or another time? Paul provided the answer, saying it will happen at the final trumpet blast:

Behold, I show you a mystery; we shall not all sleep, but we shall all be changed, in a moment, in the twinkling of an eye, at the last trump: for the trumpet shall sound, and the dead shall be raised incorruptible, and we shall be changed. For this corruptible must put on incorruption, and this mortal must put on immortality. So when this corruptible shall have put on incorruption, and this mortal shall have put on immortality, then shall be brought to pass the saying that is written, Death is swallowed up in victory. (1 Corinthians 15:51–54)

Recall Paul's mention of the trumpet sound in 1 Thessalonians: "For the Lord himself will come down from heaven, with a loud command, with the voice of the archangel and with the trumpet call of God, and the dead in Christ will rise first" (4:16).

To me, it seems clear that the reward of immortality is given to all believers at the return of Jesus and not before!

I understand it's difficult for people to reexamine strongly embedded beliefs, but when the Bible's actual words are examined without preconceived notions and assumptions, then the timetable for being "present with the Lord" points to the moment when Christ comes back to Earth and resurrects all His believers who were completely dead, asleep in their graves.

A few more notes about this: As we've read, when people die, they don't have any more thoughts. They are in the deepest, darkest sleep imaginable, oblivious to everything. That includes the passage of time. So, at the moment of death, it would seem only like an instant for believers to be with Christ whenever He returns to Earth on Resurrection Day. Centuries could pass, and it would still seem like the blink of an eye to the person who dies and comes back to life.

Altared States

There's another frequently cited passage that some claim implies people are alive in heaven as soon as they die. The apostle John saw the following in a vision:

> And when he had opened the fifth seal, I saw under the altar the souls of them that were slain for the word of God, and for the testimony which they held: And they cried with a loud voice, saying, How long, O Lord, holy and true, dost thou not judge and avenge our blood on them that dwell on the earth? And white robes were given unto every one of them; and it was said unto them, that they should rest yet for a little season, until their fellowservants also and their brethren, that should be killed as they were, should be fulfilled. (Revelation 6:9–11)

Again, let's not assume anything. The first major point is that nowhere in this passage does the word *heaven* appear. It's just not there. So why infer it? This could easily refer to an altar here on Earth.

Secondly, the word rendered *souls* is translated from the Greek word *psuche*, and can also mean "life" or "breath." When we recall how the Bible explains "the life of the flesh is in the blood" (Leviticus 17:11), the meaning becomes very different than the oft-perceived bodiless souls floating around.

The verse could be read as:

"I saw under the altar the lives of them that were slain for the word of God"

or even

"I saw under the altar the blood of them that were slain for the word of God"

It's reminiscent of the story of Cain slaying Abel, in which the Lord said, "The voice of thy brother's blood crieth unto me from the ground" (Genesis 4:10).

Abel's blood crying out from the ground is symbolic, not producing an actual sound, just as this altar scene is symbolic, leading to another point. The account of the souls under the altar is presented in a supernatural vision in a book filled with puzzling symbols. To base the belief of immortal souls on this cryptic, enigmatic section seems lacking a solid foundation.

Cross with Me

What should we say about the thief who was crucified next to Jesus? Many people think he was guaranteed a trip to heaven immediately upon his death.

The thief had just stood up for Jesus, saying Christ was being killed even though He had done nothing wrong: "And he said unto Jesus, Lord, remember me when thou comest into thy kingdom. And Jesus said unto him, Verily I say unto thee, Today shalt thou be with me in paradise" (Luke 23:42–43).

The NLT puts it this way: "And Jesus replied, 'I assure you, today you will be with me in paradise'" (v. 43).

Many cite this verse to suggest that Jesus and the thief would be in paradise—that is to say, the third heaven (2 Corinthians 12:4)—the same day they were crucified. While it may appear that way at first, there are problems with that notion.

The first has to do with punctuation. There are no commas in the original Greek, so the comma put in English before the word *today* could be placed *after* it.

Thus, the phrase "I assure you, today you will be with me in paradise" could easily be rendered, "I assure you today, you will be with me in paradise."

Jesus was not telling the thief they would both be together that same day in heaven. Instead, He was merely assuring him at that very moment that they would *eventually* be together in paradise, after the return of Jesus to Earth.

The exact word order from the original Greek language without any commas is: *Verily I say to you today with me you will be in paradise.*

But forget about punctuation for a moment. The thief simply could not have gone to heaven that day for one reason: Jesus did not go to heaven that day! Jesus was dead! He even says he was dead: "I am he that liveth, and was dead" (Revelation 1:18).

Jesus would not be raised until several days later. Regardless of whether Jesus died on a Friday and rose on a Sunday, or whether He died on a Wednesday and rose on a Saturday, He was still dead the day he was crucified. No Bible verse states Jesus went to heaven the same day he was executed. Not only that, but even after Jesus was raised from the dead, He still did not ascend to heaven immediately. How do we know? He said so.

When the resurrected Jesus appeared to Mary after she discovered the empty tomb:

> Jesus saith unto her, Touch me not; for I am not yet ascended to my Father: but go to my brethren, and say unto them, I ascend unto my Father, and your Father; and to my God, and your God. (John 20:17)

> "Don't cling to me," Jesus said, "for I haven't yet ascended to the Father. But go find my brothers and tell them that I am ascending to my Father and your Father, my God and your God." (NLT)

It appears Jesus had not yet gone to the third heaven until sometime *after* He was raised from His grave. In other words, Jesus did not go to heaven immediately, and neither did the thief crucified next to Him.

Elijah's Trip to Heaven

Another of the Bible's more significant mysteries is Elijah. Many people assume the prophet Elijah did not die a regular death but was miraculously transported to heaven while he was still alive.

It is true that Scripture tells us Elijah went to heaven; however, it's not the heaven most people have in mind.

As was pointed out earlier, there are three heavens: the sky, outer space, and God's dwelling place. Also, Jesus said no one has ever been to heaven (God's dwelling place) except for Himself. Here it is again: "No one has ever gone into heaven except the one who came from heaven—the Son of Man" (John 3:13 NIV).

These two points are crucial for understanding what really happened to Elijah.

Two Old Testament verses mention Elijah going to heaven:

When the LORD was about to take Elijah up to heaven in a whirlwind, Elijah and Elisha were traveling from Gilgal. (2 Kings 2:1 NLT)

As they were walking along and talking, suddenly a chariot of fire appeared, drawn by horses of fire. It drove between them, separating them, and Elijah was carried by a whirlwind into heaven. (2 Kings 2:11 NLT)

In this second chapter of 2 Kings, Elijah was being replaced as prophet to the king by his protégé, Elisha. The names are similar, but these are two different men.

Many who read this story automatically assume Elijah went directly to the "third heaven." When these verses are compared with other texts about the prophet, another explanation emerges that is not only plausible but likely. Elijah did not go to the heaven that is God's home but rather the "first heaven," which is the sky, and he returned to Earth in another location to live the remainder of his life. Surprisingly, there is a lot of evidence for this.

As the episode in question begins, Elijah knew that God was about to take him somewhere else. He was preparing to transfer his authority over to the younger prophet, Elisha, as the pair crossed the Jordan River: "And it came to pass, when they were gone over, that Elijah said unto Elisha, Ask what I shall do for thee, before I be taken away from thee. And Elisha said, I pray thee, let a double portion of thy spirit be upon me" (2 Kings 2:9).

Notice that Elijah did not mention becoming immortal, going to dwell with God forever, taking eternal harp lessons, or not coming back to Earth. He was only expecting to be "taken away" from Elisha. He knew he would be going somewhere. Elijah was unsure if Elisha would be granted the double portion of spirit, and that's when the whirlwind occurred.

And it came to pass, as they still went on, and talked, that, behold, there appeared a chariot of fire, and horses of fire, and parted them both asunder; and Elijah went up by a whirlwind into heaven. And Elisha saw it, and he cried, My father, my father, the chariot of Israel, and the horsemen thereof. And he saw him no more: and he took hold of his own clothes, and rent them in two pieces. (vv. 11–12)

These verses provide an incredible glimpse of the unseen world, the realm of God's angels, as it became visible and interacted with mankind. The angels were described by Elisha as horsemen riding a chariot of fire. What a dazzling sight to behold!

Elijah was brought up to the first heaven—that is, the air, the sky, the atmosphere of the Earth—courtesy of an incredible angelic ride. He did not go to the third heaven, since *Jesus said no one has gone there*. He was merely being transported to another location. The remainder of this chapter is quite telling, as other prophets-in-training expected Elijah to be brought back to Earth, and even asked Elisha if they could try to locate him.

The company of the prophets from Jericho, who were watching, said, "The spirit of Elijah is resting on Elisha." And they went to meet him and bowed to the ground before him.

"Look," they said, "we your servants have fifty able men. Let them go and look for your master. Perhaps the Spirit of the LORD has picked him up and set him down on some mountain or in some valley."

"No," Elisha replied, "do not send them." (vv. 15–16 NIV)

Elisha's attitude was that they should not bother looking, yet he nevertheless granted permission. The men hunted, but did not find Elijah. However, their lack of success does not mean Elijah had flown off into another dimension.

Elijah seems to have been flown in the air and deposited back on solid ground once he was out of eyeshot of Elisha and others. There is strong evidence that this, in fact, is the case, but that evidence is found in another book of Scripture, which is part of the reason for the confusion.

Mail from Elijah!

A few years after Elijah's whirlwind departure from Elisha, a letter of reprimand came to the evil King Jehoram, who was ruling the Southern

Kingdom of Judah (not to be confused with the Northern Kingdom of Israel). Jehoram was blasted for his wicked ways and for abandoning God. Who authored this letter? None other than Elijah the prophet! Yes, the very same Elijah who had been taken up into the air in a whirlwind years earlier!

For those who have been mystified at what became of Elijah, this part of his story comes from 2 Chronicles:

> And there came a writing to him from Elijah the prophet, saying, Thus saith the LORD God of David thy father, Because thou hast not walked in the ways of Jehoshaphat thy father, nor in the ways of Asa king of Judah, but hast walked in the way of the kings of Israel, and hast made Judah and the inhabitants of Jerusalem to go a whoring, like to the whoredoms of the house of Ahab, and also hast slain thy brethren of thy father's house, which were better than thyself: Behold, with a great plague will the LORD smite thy people, and thy children, and thy wives, and all thy goods: And thou shalt have great sickness by disease of thy bowels, until thy bowels fall out by reason of the sickness day by day. (21:12–15)

Why was God using a prophet of old to convey this message to the current king? Because Elijah had been the prophet of God during the reign of the present king's father, a king who happened to be obedient. Since Jehoram had caused the people of Judah to go "a whoring," God used Elijah to write the letter that spelled out their punishment.

The Bible does not say Elijah was dwelling with God in heaven when he wrote that letter. He did not use eternal ink on heavenly parchment with "Paradise" written on the letterhead. Elijah simply happened to be living in another area to which God had airlifted him.

But there are more texts suggesting Elijah's supernatural travel method was possible, if not typical for him.

For instance, Elijah's fellow servant of God, Obadiah, had been hiding prophets of God in secret away from the evil King Ahab. On one occasion, Obadiah said God's Holy Spirit would carry Elijah to some other location.

> But as soon as I leave you, the Spirit of the LORD will carry you away to who knows where. (1 Kings 18:12 NLT)

> I don't know where the Spirit of the LORD may carry you when I leave you. (NIV)

The other prophets who wanted to search for Elijah provide further proof. It seems they knew God's power had picked Elijah up, because they said, "Perhaps the Spirit of the LORD has picked him up and set him down on some mountain or in some valley" (2 Kings 2:16 NIV).

Air Jesus

This habit God had of airlifting people into the sky and flying them to different locations was not limited to Elijah. It happened to at least two other high-profile characters. Yes, it's in your Bible.

One case is from the New Testament. Immediately after the disciple Philip baptized an Ethiopian eunuch, Philip was supernaturally whisked away from the eunuch and was later located in another region: "And when they were come up out of the water, the Spirit of the Lord caught away Philip, that the eunuch saw him no more: and he went on his way rejoicing. But Philip was found at Azotus: and passing through he preached in all the cities, till he came to Caesarea" (Acts 8:39–40).

The second case involved the Old Testament prophet Ezekiel, as he, too, was lifted up into the sky by the power of God and miraculously transported to another location:

> [A voice said,] "Go to your people in exile and say to them, 'This is what the Sovereign LORD says!' Do this whether they listen to you or not." Then the Spirit lifted me up, and I heard a loud rumbling sound behind me . . . It was the sound of the wings of the living beings as they brushed against each other and the rumbling of their wheels beneath them. The Spirit lifted me up and took me away. I went in bitterness and turmoil, but the LORD's hold on me was strong. Then I came to the colony of Judean exiles in Tel-abib, beside the Kebar River. I sat there among them for seven days, overwhelmed. (Ezekiel 3:11–15 NLT)

And at least one other time, Elijah got somewhere in a hurry, but it was not by airlifting. Instead, God gave him the ability to run with superhuman speed. The miraculous sprint took place immediately following Elijah's victory over the prophets of Baal at Mount Carmel, as Elijah told King Ahab to get in his chariot and head for the city of Jezreel.

Then Elijah shouted, "Hurry to Ahab and tell him, 'Climb into your chariot and go back home. If you don't hurry, the rain will stop you!'" And sure enough, the sky was soon black with clouds. A heavy wind brought a terrific rainstorm, and Ahab left quickly for Jezreel. Now the LORD gave special strength to Elijah. He tucked his cloak into his belt and ran ahead of Ahab's chariot all the way to the entrance of Jezreel. (1 Kings 18:44–46 NLT)

The power of the LORD came upon Elijah and, tucking his cloak into his belt, he ran ahead of Ahab all the way to Jezreel. (v. 46 NIV)

The story sounds like something out of a Road Runner cartoon or a comic book. Elijah, boosted by a jolt of God's own turbo power, was able to run faster than a speeding chariot!

Now that the mystery of Elijah ascending into heaven has been solved, some might still question Elijah's presence in the New Testament. After all, he is said to have joined Moses and Jesus on a mountaintop in what is commonly called the "Transfiguration." The story can be found in Matthew 17:1–9; Mark 9:2–10; and Luke 9:28–36.

Here is Matthew's version, with Elijah's name rendered in its Greek version as Elias. Pay careful attention to the end of the text.

After six days Jesus taketh Peter, James, and John his brother, and bringeth them up into an high mountain apart, and was transfigured before them: and his face did shine as the sun, and his raiment was white as the light. And, behold, there appeared unto them Moses and Elias talking with him. Then answered Peter, and said unto Jesus, Lord, it is good for us to be here: if thou wilt, let us make here three tabernacles; one for thee, and one for Moses, and one for Elias. While he yet spake, behold, a bright cloud overshadowed them: and behold a voice out of the cloud, which said, This is my beloved Son, in whom I am well pleased; hear ye him. And when the disciples heard it, they fell on their face, and were sore afraid. And Jesus came and touched them, and said, Arise, and be not afraid. And when they had lifted up their eyes, they saw no man, save Jesus only. And as they came down from the mountain, Jesus charged them, saying, Tell the vision to no man, until the Son of man be risen again from the dead. (17:1–9)

Notice in the last verse, Jesus stated, *"Tell the vision to no man."* That is the key to understanding what the men had witnessed. It was not a physical, material reality but only a vision. It was a supernatural portrayal of what would be coming in the kingdom of God. It's no coincidence that the Transfiguration event occurred immediately after Jesus told His disciples that some of them would see Him in the kingdom before they died: "For the Son of man shall come in the glory of his Father with his angels; and then he shall reward every man according to his works. Verily I say unto you, there be some standing here, which shall not taste of death, till they see the Son of man coming in his kingdom" (Matthew 16:27–28).

Indeed, they received their preview of coming attractions in that Transfiguration vision.

Thus, Elijah did get to heaven—not the third heaven of God's home, but the first heaven, the sky. He was airlifted to another location on Earth, years later wrote a letter to an evil king, and eventually died, like everyone else who ever lived. But he will be resurrected in the future, when all the dead in Christ are raised to eternal life in the kingdom of God, as heaven arrives on Earth.

CHAPTER SEVEN

LET THERE BE SEX

SEX! SEX! And more sex!

Now that I have your attention, I am not referring to what is on television tonight or playing at your local theater. I am talking about the Holy Bible, a book whose sexual content would put many a romance novel or Hollywood sizzler to shame. It's time to find out what the Good Book says about the most popular subject of all time.

First, a quick note of caution: if you're easily embarrassed or offended at frank sexual discussion, you might want to skip this chapter. Strangely, though, this will probably be the most read portion of the entire book.

Just to whet your appetite, the Scriptures get down and dirty on the following subjects: sex within marriage, sex outside of marriage, sex during that time of the month, homosexuality, incest, prostitution, rape, the semen of both men and beasts, sex with animals, and even—believe it or not—homosexual relations with angels.

In the Beginning, There Was Sex

Virtually everyone who has ever heard of the Bible has been told about Adam and Eve, the first man and woman created by God. They were the original "first couple" long before there was a White House.

It's clear the two were married shortly after Eve's creation, as Scripture refers to her as Adam's wife.

And Adam said, This is now bone of my bones, and flesh of my flesh: she shall be called Woman, because she was taken out of Man. Therefore shall a man leave his father and his mother, and shall cleave unto his wife: and they shall be one flesh. And they were both naked, the man and his wife, and were not ashamed. (Genesis 2:23–25)

God created the first man and wife in the buff, completely nude. Not only that, but the first recorded instruction to men and women was not to do the dishes, mow the lawn, or take out the garbage. It was to have sex and reproduce: "So God created man in his own image, in the image of God created he him; male and female created he them. And God blessed them, and God said unto them, Be fruitful, and multiply, and replenish the earth" (Genesis 1:27–28).

Even though Adam and Eve had disobeyed God when it came to their diet, they did obey the sexual instruction (not surprisingly), and Eve became pregnant: "And Adam knew Eve his wife; and she conceived, and bare Cain, and said, I have gotten a man from the LORD. And she again bare his brother Abel" (Genesis 4:1–2).

There it is. The first case of a man having sex with his wife, and children are the result.

Yet people often wonder, "If Adam and Eve gave birth to two sons, Cain and Abel, where did the rest of the human population come from?" On an episode of *The Simpsons*, Todd and Rod Flanders, the sons of Homer Simpson's Christian neighbor, Ned Flanders, asked, "If Cain and Abel were the only children of Adam and Eve, did they make babies with their mother, or with each other?" Classic.

The question occurs, though, because people do not read the Bible enough. In the next chapter, Genesis 5:4 reveals Adam had other "sons and daughters." The sons and daughters of Adam and Eve did have conjugal relations with each other and propagated the human race. Though it was necessary at that time, sex within families would not be permissible forever, as God later laid down the law regarding sexual partners.

The Big Sex List

The book of Leviticus can be considered ground zero for regulations about sexual activity. It's packed with a laundry list of mandates from God about how to behave when it comes to carnal relations. While some people might think some of these activities are a turn-on or permissible as an "alternative lifestyle," God makes it quite clear they are definite turn-offs, using words such as *abomination* and *wickedness* when the rules are broken. It starts off with a ban on incest: "None of you shall approach to any that is near of kin to him, to uncover their nakedness. I am the LORD" (18:6).

The King James English of 1611 uses the terminology of "uncover their nakedness," but more modern Bible translations make it clear that this is about more than getting a glimpse of someone in his or her birthday suit. It's about having sex.

For instance, the New Living Translation really lays it on the line: "You must never have sexual intercourse with a close relative, for I am the Lord."

If you have trouble figuring out just who is a close relative or "near of kin," Scripture makes it easy, providing its own "Sex Rules for Dummies." They include a father, mother, another wife of a father, siblings, half siblings, grandchildren, aunts and uncles, daughters-in-law, and sisters-in-law.

And for those with an appetite to have sex with more than one person in the same family, Scripture also precludes a man having relations with a woman and her daughter, or a woman and her grandchild: "Do not have sexual intercourse with both a woman and her daughter or marry both a woman and her granddaughter, whether her son's daughter or her daughter's daughter. They are close relatives, and to do this would be a horrible wickedness" (18:17 NLT).

It also bans sex with other married people: "Moreover thou shalt not lie carnally with thy neighbour's wife, to defile thyself with her" (18:20).

And it outlaws homosexual sex:

Thou shalt not lie with mankind, as with womankind: it is abomination. (18:22)

Do not practice homosexuality; it is a detestable sin. (18:22 NLT)

In fact, God finds homosexual activity so abhorrent that He called for the death penalty for it. "If a man also lie with mankind, as he lieth with a woman, both of them have committed an abomination: they shall surely be put to death; their blood shall be upon them" (20:13).

It is not just an Old Testament prohibition. In the New Testament, the apostle Paul described homosexuality as vile affections: for even their women did change the natural use into that which is against nature: And likewise also the men, leaving the natural use of the woman, burned in their lust one toward another; men with men working that which is unseemly, and receiving in themselves that recompence of their error which was meet. (Romans 1:26–27)

Here it is in more modern language:

That is why God abandoned them to their shameful desires. Even the women turned against the natural way to have sex and instead indulged in sex with each other. (v. 26 NLT)

In the same way the men also abandoned natural relations with women and were inflamed with lust for one another. Men committed indecent acts with other men, and received in themselves the due penalty for their perversion. (v. 27 NIV)

Regarding the "due penalty for their perversion," some have speculated that this includes a sexually transmitted disease, a shortened life span, and even exclusion from the kingdom of God.

The subsequent verses in Romans feature a long list of improper behaviors of those with a "reprobate mind." Among the twenty or so items in the list are fornication (sex between unmarried partners) and being "without natural affection." It points out those "who knowing the judgment of God, that they which commit such things are worthy of death, not only do the same, but have pleasure in them that do them" (v. 32).

The NLT brings out the full meaning in modern terms: "They are fully aware of God's death penalty for those who do these things, yet they go right ahead and do them anyway. And, worse yet, they encourage others to do them, too" (v. 32).

Sex with Animals?

In addition to what I've mentioned, Scripture also says "Nay!" when it comes to having sex with animals, which is known as *bestiality*. The proof comes straight from the Almighty Himself:

Neither shalt thou lie with any beast to defile thyself therewith: neither shall any woman stand before a beast to lie down thereto: it is confusion. (Leviticus 18:23)

And if a man lie with a beast, he shall surely be put to death: and ye shall slay the beast. (Leviticus 20:15)

God also told men not to have sex with a woman while she's "unclean" with her monthly cycle: "Also thou shalt not approach unto a woman to uncover her nakedness, as long as she is put apart for her uncleanness" (Leviticus 18:19). The NLT makes this verse a bit clearer: "Do not violate a woman by having sexual intercourse with her during her period of menstrual impurity."

Despite the fact some people today think such sexual activity is hip and with the times, it's actually nothing new, as God told His people the pagan nations were engaged in it: "Defile not ye yourselves in any of these things: for in all these the nations are defiled which I cast out before you: and the land is defiled: therefore I do visit the iniquity thereof upon it, and the land itself vomiteth out her inhabitants" (Leviticus 18:24–25).

Of course, one of the Ten Commandments in Exodus 20:14 states, "Thou shalt not commit adultery." But according to the law of God, the penalty was not the silent treatment, a night on the couch, or even a nasty divorce proceeding. It was the death penalty: "And the man that committeth adultery with another man's wife, even he that committeth adultery with his neighbour's wife, the adulterer and the adulteress shall surely be put to death" (Leviticus 20:10).

Even more surprising is that people aren't required to actually have sex with someone to be guilty of committing sexual sin. Just looking at someone other than your spouse with the desire to have sex is bad enough. Jesus made that clear in the New Testament: "Ye have heard that it was said by them of old time, Thou shalt not commit adultery: But I say unto you, That whosoever looketh on a woman to lust after her hath committed adultery with her already in his heart" (Matthew 5:27–28).

This is not to say God has a problem with all sexual activity. He just wants it to be in the confines of marriage. "Marriage should be honored by all, and the marriage bed kept pure, for God will judge the adulterer and all the sexually immoral" (Hebrews 13:4 NIV).

The Breast of the Story

For those who have never investigated the matter, Scripture is filled with sexual terminology, from body parts to activities.

For instance, the word *breasts* is found twenty-seven times in the King James translation. That's four more instances than the phrases "God the Father" and "God our Father" combined! And some of the references celebrate women's breasts in a positive, sexual manner.

King Solomon had plenty to say about them in Proverbs and Song of Songs, as he glorified physical love between a man and a woman.

Let thy fountain be blessed: and rejoice with the wife of thy youth. Let her be as the loving hind and pleasant roe; let her breasts satisfy thee at all times; and be thou ravished always with her love. And why wilt thou, my son, be ravished with a strange woman, and embrace the bosom of a stranger? (Proverbs 5:18–20)

A bundle of myrrh is my well-beloved unto me; he shall lie all night betwixt my breasts. (Song of Songs 1:13)

Your breasts are like twin fawns of a gazelle, feeding among the lilies. (Song of Songs 4:5 NLT)

We have a little sister, and she hath no breasts: what shall we do for our sister in the day when she shall be spoken for? (Song of Songs 8:8)

I am a wall, and my breasts like towers: then was I in his eyes as one that found favour. (Song of Songs 8:10)

Of course, there are sex-related terms that have more negative connotations. For example, *fornication* is mentioned thirty-six times; *adultery*, forty; *harlot*, forty; *whore*, fourteen; and *whoredom* twenty-two times in the King James Bible of 1611.

Here are some classic references:

What? know ye not that he which is joined to an harlot is one body? for two, saith he, shall be one flesh. (1 Corinthians 6:16)

Do not prostitute thy daughter, to cause her to be a whore; lest the land fall to whoredom, and the land become full of wickedness. (Leviticus 19:29)

Marriage is honourable in all, and the bed undefiled; but whoremongers and adulterers God will judge. (Hebrews 13:4)

Flee fornication. Every sin that a man doeth is without the body; but he that committeth fornication sinneth against his own body. (1 Corinthians 6:18)

It is reported commonly that there is fornication among you, and such fornication as is not so much as named among the Gentiles, that one should have his father's wife. (1 Corinthians 5.1)

As seen in this last verse, the apostle Paul was severely critical of a Christian man who was having sex with his father's wife.

Seedy Talk

The Bible, even in the archaic English of the seventeenth century, also gets quite descriptive about some sexual terms and activities.

Consider this passage regarding semen: "And if any man's seed of copulation go out from him, then he shall wash all his flesh in water, and be unclean until the even. And every garment, and every skin, whereon is the seed of copulation, shall be washed with water, and be unclean until the even. The woman also with whom man shall lie with seed of copulation, they shall both bathe themselves in water, and be unclean until the even" (Leviticus 15:16–18).

Another fascinating Bible story recounts how Judah's son, Onan, was instructed to marry and have sexual intercourse with his sister-in-law after God killed her wicked first husband. When the crucial time came, Onan did not fulfill his duty. "But Onan was not willing to have a child who would not be his own heir. So whenever he had intercourse with Tamar, he spilled the semen on the ground to keep her from having a baby who would belong to his brother. But the LORD considered it a wicked thing for Onan to deny a child to his dead brother. So the LORD took Onan's life, too" (Genesis 38:9–10 NLT).

God actually killed Onan for not providing the "family seed" to his brother's wife so she could continue the line of her dead husband.

Other graphic sexual language is found in Ezekiel, where God tells the story of two sisters—symbolically the kingdoms of Israel and Judah—who became sexually active in their youth, had their breasts fondled as virgins, and later plunged headlong into sin as they lusted after lovers who ejaculated like large animals.

> The word of the LORD came to me: "Son of man, there were two women, daughters of the same mother. They became prostitutes in Egypt, engaging in prostitution from their youth. In that land their breasts were fondled and their virgin bosoms caressed . . . She did not give up the prostitution she began in Egypt, when during her youth men slept with her, caressed her virgin bosom and poured out their lust upon her . . . There she lusted after her lovers, whose genitals were like those of donkeys and whose emission was like that of horses. (23:1–3, 8, 20 NIV)

I am making an educated guess that many longtime churchgoers had no idea the Bible refers to the ejaculate of horses.

Rules of Rape

The Bible mentions rape numerous times, describing a variety of penalties that depended on such specific circumstances as whether or not the woman being raped had been engaged to be married, and if she resisted her assailant.

> Suppose a man meets a young woman, a virgin who is engaged to be married, and he has sexual intercourse with her. If this happens within a town, you must take both of them to the gates of the town and stone them to death. The woman is guilty because she did not scream for help. The man must die because he violated another man's wife. In this way, you will cleanse the land of evil.
>
> But if the man meets the engaged woman out in the country, and he rapes her, then only the man should die. Do nothing to the young woman; she has committed no crime worthy of death. This case is similar to that of someone who attacks and murders a neighbor. Since the man

raped her out in the country, it must be assumed that she screamed, but there was no one to rescue her.

If a man is caught in the act of raping a young woman who is not engaged, he must pay fifty pieces of silver to her father. Then he must marry the young woman because he violated her, and he will never be allowed to divorce her. (Deuteronomy 22:23–29 NLT)

Even Dinah, the daughter of Jacob and Leah, became a rape victim in the first book of the Old Testament. "One day Dinah, Leah's daughter, went to visit some of the young women who lived in the area. But when the local prince, Shechem son of Hamor the Hivite, saw her, he took her and raped her" (Genesis 34:1–2 NLT).

And in at least one instance, the Bible notes a situation where sexual activity might have been expected but never took place. The book of 1 Kings describes how an elderly King David could not stay warm at night in bed, no matter how many covers he had on him. The solution was not to find thicker blankets or even light a fire, but to hunt down the most luscious virgin in the nation—someone with whom the king could snuggle, but not have intercourse (I kid you not).

Now King David was very old, and no matter how many blankets covered him, he could not keep warm. So his advisers told him, "We will find a young virgin who will wait on you and be your nurse. She will lie in your arms and keep you warm." So they searched throughout the country for a beautiful girl, and they found Abishag from Shunem and brought her to the king. The girl was very beautiful, and she waited on the king and took care of him. But the king had no sexual relations with her. (1:1–4 NLT)

Viagra, of course, would not be invented for another few thousand years.

Gay Sex with Angels

"Gay sex with angels!" It sounds like those over-the-top headlines on a cable news channel or the front page of the tabloids. Or it could be another episode on the *Jerry Springer Show*.

Gay sex with angels? *In the Bible?* Am I serious? Yes. The Bible actually records an event where homosexual men demanded to have sexual relations with angels who appeared in the form of men. It took place in the ancient city of Sodom, moments before the city was destroyed for the wickedness of its inhabitants.

The story is found in the nineteenth chapter of Genesis, and concerns Lot, Abraham's nephew.

> And there came two angels to Sodom at even; and Lot sat in the gate of Sodom: and Lot seeing them rose up to meet them; and he bowed himself with his face toward the ground; and he said, Behold now, my lords, turn in, I pray you, into your servant's house, and tarry all night, and wash your feet, and ye shall rise up early, and go on your ways. And they said, Nay; but we will abide in the street all night. And he pressed upon them greatly; and they turned in unto him, and entered into his house; and he made them a feast, and did bake unleavened bread, and they did eat. (vv. 1–3)

In the previous chapter, the angels were sent on a reconnaissance mission from God to see Sodom and Gomorrah's wicked behavior for themselves. If they found ten righteous citizens, the region would be spared from destruction by God. "And the LORD said, Because the cry of Sodom and Gomorrah is great, and because their sin is very grievous; I will go down now, and see whether they have done altogether according to the cry of it, which is come unto me; and if not, I will know" (18:20–21).

A few chapters earlier, the author noted, "But the men of Sodom were wicked and sinners before the LORD exceedingly" (13:13).

The angels, who looked like typical human men, arrived in the evening and ate a meal prepared by Lot.

"But before they lay down, the men of the city, even the men of Sodom, compassed the house round, both old and young, all the people from every quarter: and they called unto Lot, and said unto him, Where are the men which came in to thee this night? bring them out unto us, that we may know them" (19:4–5).

Surprisingly, it was not one or two men who sought out the angels but virtually the entire male population, "both old and young," who came "from every quarter." They surrounded Lot's house and ordered him to send out the men (again, really angels) so they could have sex with them.

The King James translation of the Bible uses the phrase "that we may know them." This, however, is a euphemism for knowing them carnally, rather than being acquainted with them casually. In Genesis, Adam "knew" his wife, Eve, and she conceived. More modern versions nail the precise meaning by translating it as having sex.

> They shouted to Lot, "Where are the men who came to spend the night with you? Bring them out so we can have sex with them." (v. 5 NLT)

> They called to Lot, "Where are the men who came to you tonight? Bring them out to us so that we can have sex with them." (NIV)

The subsequent verses also make it clear that Lot realized the men of the city wanted to engage in sexual relations with the angels. "And Lot went out at the door unto them, and shut the door after him, and said, I pray you, brethren, do not so wickedly" (vv. 6–7).

Instead, Lot proposed a stunning alternative of his own, offering up his own virgin daughters. Lot told them,

> Behold now, I have two daughters which have not known man; let me, I pray you, bring them out unto you, and do ye to them as is good in your eyes: only unto these men do nothing; for therefore came they under the shadow of my roof. (v. 8)

> [Lot said,] "Look, I have two daughters who have never slept with a man. Let me bring them out to you, and you can do what you like with them. But don't do anything to these men, for they have come under the protection of my roof." (v. 8 NIV)

That's astounding. Lot offered up his daughters in lieu of his angelic guests, despite not being sure whether or not his girls would even be returned alive. Nevertheless, he sought to protect the angels, as he was certain they had been sent from God.

Meanwhile, Sodom's men apparently had no interest in the opportunity to have sex with the virgin girls. They ignored Lot's offer and continued to make their demands to have sex with the angelic fellows, blasting Lot for suggesting their desire to have sex with other men was "wicked" and rebuking him for acting as their judge. "'Stand back!' they shouted. 'Who do you think you are? We let you settle among us, and now you are trying to tell us what to do! We'll treat you far worse than those other men!' And they lunged at Lot and began breaking down the door" (v. 9 NLT).

The entire male population of this ancient city surrounded Lot, his wife, virgin daughters, and two angels and readied to smash down the door. In their lust, they said they would deal worse with Lot than they would with the angelic men, reinforcing the point that they were not interested in being acquaintances with the new faces in town.

The angels then rescued Lot from the attacking homosexuals, who all received something they did not expect. "But the two angels reached out and pulled Lot in and bolted the door. Then they blinded the men of Sodom so they couldn't find the doorway" (vv. 10–11 NLT).

The homosexuals, now struck with blindness, could find neither Lot nor the angelic guests for their assault. Blindness was only the beginning of their problems, though. God soon destroyed the cities and burned them to death: "Then the LORD rained down burning sulfur on Sodom and Gomorrah—from the LORD out of the heavens" (v. 24 NIV).

A "Lot" of Sex

Immediately after the destruction of Sodom and Gomorrah, the Bible returns to a story about sex—the incestuous kind—between Lot and his two virgin daughters. Lot's wife had been turned to a pillar of salt for disobeying the angels' instruction not to look back, and the girls apparently thought it was their patriotic duty to repopulate the planet.

> Lot and his two daughters left Zoar and settled in the mountains, for he was afraid to stay in Zoar. He and his two daughters lived in a cave. One day the older daughter said to the younger, "Our father is old, and there is no man around here to lie with us, as is the custom all over the earth. Let's get our father to drink wine and then lie with him and preserve our family line through our father." That night they got their father to drink wine, and the older daughter went in and lay with him. He was not aware of it when she lay down or when she got up. The next day the older daughter said to the younger, "Last night I lay with my father. Let's get him to drink wine again tonight, and you go in and lie with him so we can preserve our family line through our father." So they got their father

to drink wine that night also, and the younger daughter went and lay with him. Again he was not aware of it when she lay down or when she got up. So both of Lot's daughters became pregnant by their father. (vv. 30–36 NIV)

There is no shortage of sexual matters in the Bible. From the very first instruction to be fruitful and multiply, to warnings about harmful behaviors, Scripture is replete with frank discussion about sex.

Could that be one of the reasons it has been the best-selling book throughout the ages?

CHAPTER EIGHT

THE DUMB ASS OF THE BIBLE

HOW WOULD YOU like for all eternity to be known as the "dumb ass" of the Bible?

Just imagine if for centuries you had to claim the title bestowed upon you in 1611 by the translators of the King James Version. It's no joke. The Word of God has dubbed a character in its pages a true "dumb ass."

And who is the recipient of such a unique, if not ignominious, title? Was it Adam or Eve, who disobeyed God by eating from the tree they were instructed to avoid? Was it Cain, Adam's firstborn son, who killed his brother? Could it have been Judas, one of the original apostles of Jesus, who betrayed the Son of God? Or perhaps Satan himself, who was first to rebel against God?

All of those would certainly be fitting, but none can claim the official title of the Bible's "dumb ass." That belongs solely to a character mentioned in both the Old and New Testaments: the donkey that spoke with a human voice.

If you don't believe me, read 2 Peter, where Peter describes the evil people of his day:

Which have forsaken the right way, and are gone astray, following the way of Balaam the son of Bosor, who loved the wages of unrighteousness;

but was rebuked for his iniquity: the dumb ass speaking with man's voice forbad the madness of the prophet. (2:15–16)

Balaam's mute donkey, or as the Bible puts it, his "dumb ass," spoke with the voice of a man. A number of other Bible translations, including the Revised Standard Version of 1952, the Noah Webster Version of 1833, the Robert Young Literal Translation of 1898, the J. N. Darby Translation of 1890, and the American Standard Version of 1901, all use the same phrase to describe the beast without speech as a "dumb ass."

If I Could Talk to the Animals

The story of the "dumb ass" reveals an often overlooked aspect of Scripture: animals had meaningful discussions with human beings! It sounds bizarre, but just think about how children watch cartoon characters such as Bugs Bunny or Daffy Duck. The animals all talk, and no one thinks twice about it. The same thing is recorded in the Bible, and in the first few pages at that.

The first instance of an animal talking is in the garden of Eden, the newly created home of Adam and Eve. A serpent spoke with Eve, questioning her about her dietary restrictions from God.

Now the serpent was more subtil than any beast of the field which the LORD God had made. And he said unto the woman, Yea, hath God said, Ye shall not eat of every tree of the garden? And the woman said unto the serpent, We may eat of the fruit of the trees of the garden: But of the fruit of the tree which is in the midst of the garden, God hath said, Ye shall not eat of it, neither shall ye touch it, lest ye die. (Genesis 3:1–3)

There is no indication that Eve was surprised to hear an animal speaking. Perhaps she took the voice for granted. After all, she hadn't been around very long and didn't have much experience to which she could compare this one. The subject matter with which the serpent dealt was also highly sophisticated and profound: he was questioning the instructions God had given Adam and Eve.

Of course, this serpent was not just any reptile. Revelation suggests it was Satan. "And the great dragon was cast out, that old serpent, called the Devil, and Satan, which deceiveth the whole world" (12:9).

Its conversation with Eve continued, and the serpent uttered the first lie in the Bible.

> And the serpent said unto the woman, Ye shall not surely die: For God doth know that in the day ye eat thereof, then your eyes shall be opened, and ye shall be as gods, knowing good and evil. (Genesis 3:4–5)

Most people know the rest of the story, as both Eve and her husband succumbed to the serpent's temptation and ate the forbidden fruit. The couple was banished from the garden and ended up dying years later.

Since the serpent doing the talking was really the devil, many might not consider it to be a typical beast.

However, the serpent is not the only talking animal in Scripture. The famous "dumb ass" story occurs in the book of Numbers, when the Israelites were finally headed toward the promised land after wandering in the desert for decades.

Dumb, but Not Stupid

The person at the center of the tale is Balaam, a man sought out by the Moabite king named Balak. The pagan monarch had been fretting over the pending arrival of the Israelites and thus wanted to put a curse on them. According to the biblical record, God interrupted Balaam's mission and told him not to curse the Israelites, for they had been blessed.

Balaam initially followed God's instructions, but he was not completely obedient. He began traveling on his donkey before he was supposed to, and as a result, an angel appeared and blocked the route of Balaam and his dumb ass.

> And the ass saw the angel of the LORD standing in the way, and his sword drawn in his hand: and the ass turned aside out of the way, and went into the field: and Balaam smote the ass, to turn her into the way. But the angel of the LORD stood in a path of the vineyards, a wall being on this side, and a wall on that side. And when the ass saw the angel of the LORD, she thrust herself unto the wall, and crushed Balaam's foot against the wall: and he smote her again. And the angel of the LORD went further, and stood in a narrow place, where was no way to turn either to the

right hand or to the left. And when the ass saw the angel of the LORD, she fell down under Balaam: and Balaam's anger was kindled, and he smote the ass with a staff. (Numbers 22:23–27)

Surprisingly, the invisible spirit world is apparently quite visible to this animal. While it's not clear from the account whether animals can see angels all the time, in this case the creature was cognizant of the angel's presence. Balaam, who initially could not see the angel, could not understand why his four-legged ride acted so strangely. But when he began beating the animal, an intelligent, human-sounding voice suddenly came from the mouth of the creature.

> Then the LORD caused the donkey to speak. "What have I done to you that deserves your beating me these three times?" it asked Balaam.
>
> "Because you have made me look like a fool!" Balaam shouted. "If I had a sword with me, I would kill you!"
>
> "But I am the same donkey you always ride on," the donkey answered. "Have I ever done anything like this before?"
>
> "No," he admitted. (vv. 28–30 NLT)

This story has several fascinating aspects. First, just as in Eve's conversation with the serpent, there is no indication that Balaam was surprised to hear an animal talking to him. But unlike the story in Genesis, the "personality" uttering the words here seems to be that of the donkey itself. The text says God had caused the dumb ass to speak, but the animal voiced its opinion as if it retained its memory as a donkey. It asked Balaam why he was beating it and recounted their personal history together, reminding the man that it had never acted in such a strange fashion previously.

The donkey did not utter any further words, as the conversation shifted to one between Balaam and God's angel.

> Then the LORD opened Balaam's eyes, and he saw the angel of the LORD standing in the roadway with a drawn sword in his hand. Balaam fell face down on the ground before him. "Why did you beat your donkey those three times?" the angel of the LORD demanded. "I have come to block your way because you are stubbornly resisting me. Three times the donkey saw me and shied away; otherwise, I would certainly have killed you

by now and spared the donkey." Then Balaam confessed to the angel of the LORD, "I have sinned. I did not realize you were standing in the road to block my way. I will go back home if you are against my going." (vv. 31–34 NLT)

The story is nothing short of amazing, and it could easily be used as a starting point to help children become acquainted with the Bible. Whenever kids see animals in cartoons or movies having a conversation, you can simply point out the Bible was the first place animals are shown talking!

CHAPTER NINE

HEMORRHOIDS HEARD IN HEAVEN

HOLY HEMORRHOIDS! Does the Bible really talk about hemorrhoids? You bet your sore tush it does.

I suspect many people are itching to read this chapter. Even those who thought they knew virtually everything there is to know about the Bible are inflamed with curiosity to see where I'm going with this one. Take a seat (that is, if it's comfortable to do so), because this chapter has a soothing treatment on the subject of hemorrhoids from the pages of Scripture.

Hemorrhoids are discussed eight times in eight separate verses. Probably the reason most people are unaware of the hemorrhoidal issue is that their eyes glaze over at the word in their King James Versions, which employ an archaic English word for hemorrhoids: *emerods*. It sounds similar to our modern pronunciation, but it was spelled differently in the year 1611.

In fact, several Bible translations, including the J. N. Darby version of 1890, actually use *hemorrhoids* instead of *emerods*. According to the *Gesenius Lexicon*, the Hebrew word *t'chor*, rendered "emerods" in the Bible, is defined as "tumours of the anus, hæmorrhoidal mariscœ, protruding from the anus."

The Itch That Wouldn't Stop

The first mention of hemorrhoids (emerods) in the Bible comes in the twenty-eighth chapter of Deuteronomy, where God listed the blessings for obeying His commandments, and the curses if the people rebelled. The list of curses is horrendous, as incredible evils would befall the Israelites who chose to disobey.

Among the problems mentioned in the warnings were—here it is, folks—hemorrhoids! "The LORD will smite thee with the botch of Egypt, and with the emerods, and with the scab, and with the itch, whereof thou canst not be healed" (v. 27).

Interesting how God put hemorrhoids and "the itch" in the same sentence, huh?

The remaining references appear in 1 Samuel, as God actually inflicted this plague on a nation. The victims were the Philistines—the longtime enemies of ancient Israel—who were living in a region called Ashdod.

The Philistines had come into possession of the famous ark of the covenant, God's holy box that carried the Ten Commandments. God was not pleased that these worshippers of the pagan god Dagon possessed the Ark, so he put the heat on them with a flaring case of hemorrhoids: "But the hand of the LORD was heavy upon them of Ashdod, and he destroyed them, and smote them with emerods, even Ashdod and the coasts thereof" (5:6).

Again, the Darby Translation comes right out and uses the word *hemorrhoids*: "And the hand of Jehovah was heavy upon them of Ashdod, and he laid them waste, and smote them with hemorrhoids,—Ashdod and its borders."

The Bible does not casually mention this affliction in one verse and leave it alone. It goes out of its way to point out that the Philistines had a big problem in their pants: "And it was so, that . . . the hand of the LORD was against the city with a very great destruction: and he smote the men of the city, both small and great, and they had emerods in their secret parts" (v. 9).

Those living in Ashdod knew possessing the ark of the covenant was the reason for their ailment, so they brought the Ark to another town called Ekron. But the problem persisted, with some Philistines being killed by God while others were struck by a wicked case of hemorrhoids. "And the men that died not were smitten with the hemorrhoids; and the cry of the city went up to heaven" (v. 12 DARBY).

This was likely the worst case of hemorrhoidal hysteria in history, with people shrieking so loudly from pain that their voices were heard in heaven. But just when it seems the story couldn't become any more "earthy," it does, as those in agony go to astounding measures to alleviate their suffering. Preparation H, of course, would not be available for several millennia.

Chapter 6 of 1 Samuel tells us the Ark had been in the Philistines' possession for seven agonizing months. The Philistines could not stand the itching, swelling, and bleeding any longer. Upon meeting with their priests and diviners, the Philistines decided they would return the Ark, along with the gift of a trespass offering, which is basically a way to pay off debt.

Five Golden 'rhoids

What sort of gift did the Philistines send to appease God almighty and hopefully alleviate the hemorrhoid epidemic?

It sounds like a skit on a grotesque comedy show, but the Philistines made golden images of those very hemorrhoids and sent them to the Israelites with the Ark. They also included golden images of mice. Here's the King James Version:

> Then said they, What shall be the trespass offering which we shall return to him? They answered, Five golden emerods, and five golden mice, according to the number of the lords of the Philistines: for one plague was on you all, and on your lords. Wherefore ye shall make images of your emerods, and images of your mice that mar the land; and ye shall give glory unto the God of Israel: peradventure he will lighten his hand from off you, and from off your gods, and from off your land. (vv. 4–5)

And the Darby Translation:

> Then they said, What is the trespass offering which we shall return to him? And they said, Five golden hemorrhoids, and five golden mice, the number of the lords of the Philistines; for one plague is upon them all, and upon your lords. And ye shall make images of your hemorrhoids, and images of your mice that destroy the land, and give glory to the God of Israel: perhaps he will lighten his hand from off you, and from off your gods, and from off your land.

This story reminds me of "The Twelve Days of Christmas," where gifts are given each day. As the song puts it, "On the fifth day of Christmas, my true love sent to me, five golden rings." Only in this case, it was five golden 'rhoids.

Of course, they chose five golden hemorrhoids instead of a dozen, or fifty, because each one represented one of the five regional rulers of the Philistines: "And these are the golden emerods which the Philistines returned for a trespass offering unto the LORD; for Ashdod one, for Gaza one, for Askelon one, for Gath one, for Ekron one" (v. 17).

To make a long story short, the Philistines loaded their golden hemorrhoid images on a cart along with the ark of the covenant and tied two cows to it. "And they laid the ark of the LORD upon the cart, and the coffer with the mice of gold and the images of their emerods" (v. 11).

Ultimately, the cows, with only divine providence guiding them, made their way back to the territory of the Israelites.

It's one of the least known—and strangest—stories in the entire Bible. Of course, the passages should be highlighted in order to help ease the itch to find them again.

CHAPTER TEN

ONE BAD APPLE DON'T SPOIL THE WHOLE BUNCH

IN COUNTLESS STORIES, songs, paintings, poems, photographs, advertisements, and films, the apple is portrayed as the forbidden fruit of Eden. It's often associated with evil and with the fall of Adam and Eve into sin and death. Why? Because many people assume it's the one food God told the first human beings never to eat.

But before you empty out your fruit bowl or cancel your apple-picking trip to the orchard, chew on this: the Bible does *not* say Adam and Eve ate an apple.

We *do* know for certain that the fruit was a product of the tree of knowledge of good and evil:

> And out of the ground made the Lord God to grow every tree that is pleasant to the sight, and good for food; the tree of life also in the midst of the garden, and the tree of knowledge of good and evil . . . And the Lord God commanded the man, saying, Of every tree of the garden thou mayest freely eat: But of the tree of the knowledge of good and evil, thou shalt not eat of it: for in the day that thou eatest thereof thou shalt surely die. (Genesis 2:9, 16–17)

The word *apple* is never mentioned. Yet people continue to suggest the serpent used an apple to tempt Eve:

And the woman said unto the serpent, We may eat of the fruit of the trees of the garden: But of the fruit of the tree which is in the midst of the garden, God hath said, Ye shall not eat of it, neither shall ye touch it, lest ye die. And the serpent said unto the woman, Ye shall not surely die: For God doth know that in the day ye eat thereof, then your eyes shall be opened, and ye shall be as gods, knowing good and evil. And when the woman saw that the tree was good for food, and that it was pleasant to the eyes, and a tree to be desired to make one wise, she took of the fruit thereof, and did eat, and gave also unto her husband with her; and he did eat. And the eyes of them both were opened, and they knew that they were naked; and they sewed fig leaves together, and made themselves aprons. (Genesis 3:2–7)

Some have speculated that since the account mentions fig leaves, a fig brought the fall. We can't be certain. Eve's downfall could have come from an apple, of course—or a banana, orange, pear, peach, kiwifruit, or kumquat, for that matter. Maybe Eve was overcome with mango madness or a desire for passion fruit. Fitting, huh? The garden of Eden might have even contained fruit that no longer exists.

So where did this idea of apples being the forbidden fruit originate? There are several possibilities.

The first simply asserts that the original forbidden fruit was indeed an apple. Whether it was a golden delicious, Granny Smith, or something more like a McIntosh is anyone's guess. Ancient paganism could have perpetuated the idea of the apple as well. In Greek mythology, Gaia, who is also known as Mother Earth or Mother Nature, presented a tree with golden apples to Zeus and his bride, Hera, on their wedding day. As in the Genesis story, the tree grew in a garden, guarded by a serpent that never slept.

Next, historians and etymologists have noted that the word *apple* is a term applied generically to almost any fruit, no matter its exact type. Thus, different kinds of produce can be and have been called apples. Look at a pineapple, which is a far cry from a Red Delicious apple. The pineapple's name came about because it's a fruit (generically called an apple) that resembles a pinecone. Pomegranates are literally "apples with many seeds." Even a potato is an "apple of the earth" when you consider its French name, *pomme de terre*. The word *pomme* derives from the Latin *pomum*, translated as both "fruit" and "apple."

If that's not enough to spice up your brain, there's even more to the language game.

It's interesting to note that another Latin word for apple, *malus*, is also the Latin word for evil. *Malus* is where we get the modern English word *malice*. So for centuries, when people using the Latin Bible learned about the tree of knowledge of good and evil, the text included a pun on the words for apple and evil. The text referring to the "tree of knowledge of good and evil" could playfully be understood as "the tree of knowledge of good and apple."

Apples are actually mentioned in the Bible. The word *apple* is found eight times in the King James Version, while the plural *apples* is found three times. When mentioned in Scripture, the word *apple* never bears a negative connotation. In fact, the word is used in a very positive light.

Here are a few examples:

A word fitly spoken is like apples of gold in pictures of silver. (Proverbs 25:11)

Oh, feed me with your love—your "raisins" and your "apples"—for I am utterly lovesick! (Song of Songs 2:5 NLT)

I said, "I will climb up into the palm tree and take hold of its branches." Now may your breasts be like grape clusters, and the scent of your breath like apples. (Song of Songs 7:8 NLT)

Keep me as the apple of the eye, hide me under the shadow of thy wings. (Psalm 17:8)

Keep my commandments, and live; and my law as the apple of thine eye. (Proverbs 7:2)

Apple lovers can rejoice! When it comes to what's written in the Bible regarding their favorite fruit, it's all good.

CHAPTER ELEVEN

THE LIVE FOREVER DIET

EAT ANYTHING you want, and still drop twenty pounds!"

"Chomp away your ugly chub with the fabulous flab-melter pill!"

"Juice everything from eggplants to eggshells!"

We live in an age when dieting has become an obsession for many people—especially those in the advertising industry who come up with catchy slogans to cash in on everyone's desire for a long, healthy life. The ads make outrageous claims, but I bet the ad execs have never imagined this one: "Eat and live forever!" Certainly no one would dare to make an advertisement suggesting people could eat a certain food and never die.

But the "Live Forever Diet," as I've dubbed it, is indeed a reality, found in the pages of the Holy Bible. There is no need to dig deep to locate it, as it shows up in the initial chapters of the Good Book. It's associated with one of the most extraordinary stories in all of Scripture.

Off the Menu

The story involves Adam and Eve, the first man and woman created by God. They had been placed in the garden of Eden, which provided all they needed for a satisfying, happy life. They did not even have to worry about laundry, because they did not know about clothing. I think we can also safely infer that since they were naked, God kept their climate perfectly controlled, and they never needed to adjust the thermostat.

As far as their menu was concerned, Adam and Eve enjoyed a large variety of foods. They had the green light to eat from any tree in the garden—with one exception:

And out of the ground made the LORD God to grow every tree that is pleasant to the sight, and good for food; the tree of life also in the midst of the garden, and the tree of knowledge of good and evil . . . And the LORD God commanded the man, saying, Of every tree of the garden thou mayest freely eat: But of the tree of the knowledge of good and evil, thou shalt not eat of it: for in the day that thou eatest thereof thou shalt surely die. (Genesis 2:9, 16–17)

With the exception of this single tree, God wanted Adam and Eve to eat from any tree in the garden—including the tree of life.

If Adam and Eve ate from the tree of knowledge of good and evil, they would die. The couple, deceived by a serpent later identified as the devil, did indeed eat from the prohibited tree, and they eventually died.

What of the Live Forever Diet I have mentioned? If Adam and Eve had chosen the correct path and avoided the knowledge tree, instead eating from the tree of life, they would indeed have lived forever. The proof is in God's reaction to the couple's disobedience:

And the LORD God said, Behold, the man is become as one of us, to know good and evil: and now, lest he put forth his hand, and take also of the tree of life, and eat, and live for ever: Therefore the LORD God sent him forth from the garden of Eden, to till the ground from whence he was taken. (3:22–23)

God acknowledged that mankind suddenly knew good and evil, but He specifically did not want His creations to eat from the tree of life after they had disobeyed, and thus inherit the ability to live forever. Read those two Bible verses again slowly and grasp what they are shouting. Here is the key line: "And now, lest he put forth his hand, and take also of the tree of life, and eat, and live for ever . . ."

The New Living Translation confirms that this is not just some strange idea in the archaic English of the seventeenth century: "Then the LORD God said, 'The people have become as we are, knowing everything, both good and

evil. What if they eat the fruit of the tree of life? Then they will live forever!'"
(v. 22)

And the New International Version concurs: "And the Lord God said,
'The man has now become like one of us, knowing good and evil. He must
not be allowed to reach out his hand and take also from the tree of life and
eat, and live forever.'"

Look it up in your own Bible, because most translations say the same
thing. Even Jerome's Latin Vulgate Bible, completed in the year 405, uses the
phrase *vivat in aeternum*. You do not have to be a Latin expert to see the
words "live in eternity."

If Adam and Eve had eaten from the tree of life, they would have lived
forever. Eternal life is apparently the natural result of eating from the tree of
life. Thus, it makes good sense that God named it the "tree of life."

The text does not give enough detail for us to know whether it required
one helping or many to gain everlasting life, but we see God taking rapid,
drastic action to completely remove Adam and Eve from the location where
the tree of life grew. Now that they were sinners, he did not want them to
live forever.

Living Forever: Plan B

But the story does not end there. Not only did God boot Adam and Eve
from the garden, but He also took a fascinating extra step to make sure they
and their offspring would not have another chance to eat from the tree of
life. He stationed supernatural guards—high-ranking angels known as *cherubim*—at Eden's edge to prevent any human's return: "And he placed at the
east of the garden of Eden Cherubims, and a flaming sword which turned
every way, to keep the way of the tree of life" (v. 24).

These angels were armed! Their weapon served, apparently, as a visible
deterrent warning against unauthorized entry.

The end of verse 24 reveals that God in fact saved the pair from a much
larger problem than their initial rebellion and resulting punishment. And that
bigger problem is the opposite of living forever. It is being dead forever.

Consider this: the banishment from Eden took place to protect human
beings. The armed angelic guards were put on duty "to keep the way of the
tree of life."

Other translations pick up on this guarding mission: "After he drove the man out, he placed on the east side of the Garden of Eden cherubim and a flaming sword flashing back and forth to guard the way to the tree of life" (v. 24 NIV).

They were preventing men and women from becoming sinners who would never die.

The angels helped set the stage for the future salvation of the human race. Their assignment was the commencement of God's Plan B. That Plan B involved the Savior of mankind, Jesus Christ, leaving His heavenly home, living as a man like Adam, but resisting the devil's temptations and reclaiming all that God had intended for Adam and his descendants when He created them: eternal life and dominion over every created thing. The guardian angels of Eden had the serious responsibility of preventing access to the source of everlasting life, the original fountain of youth.

As an aside, it's possible, though not specified in the Bible text, that the legends about a fountain of youth originated at Eden. Has it inspired other tales as well, including quests for treasure guarded by dragons or other mysterious creatures? It's pure speculation, but interesting to consider. Remember, the angels at Eden were indeed guarding a fantastic, almost unspeakable treasure—a treasure that could make people live forever!

The exact phrase "the tree of life" occurs only in the two books at opposite ends of the Bible: Genesis and Revelation. After the angels were posted to guard the way of the tree of life, thousands of years passed before the subject was brought up in connection with the return of Jesus Christ to Earth:

> He that hath an ear, let him hear what the Spirit saith unto the churches; to him that overcometh will I give to eat of the tree of life, which is in the midst of the paradise of God. (Revelation 2:7)

> In the midst of the street of it, and on either side of the river, was there the tree of life, which bare twelve manner of fruits, and yielded her fruit every month: and the leaves of the tree were for the healing of the nations. (Revelation 22:2)

> Blessed are they that do his commandments, that they may have right to the tree of life, and may enter in through the gates into the city. (Revelation 22:14)

Here we learn more details about the tree of life. It is an actual tree that produces twelve kinds of fruit—a new crop every month. Its leaves are used for the healing of nations. God may have created more than one of these trees, since the passage places them not only in the midst of the street but also on either side of the river, though it could be also a single massive tree, the branches of which have an enormous expanse.

While some Bible readers might believe the tree of life is merely a literary device symbolizing eternal life, the Bible makes it clear it is an actual tree, and just as real as the tree of knowledge of good and evil. God intended people to eat of the fruit of the tree of life, as He told Adam and Eve, "Of every tree of the garden thou mayest freely eat."

Since the events of Genesis, no one has ever conclusively found where the garden of Eden and the tree of life were located. But when we take the book of Revelation at face value, it's clear that the tree of life will be present in God's future paradise, and those who have overcome and follow God's commandments will be allowed to eat from it.

CHAPTER TWELVE

NOAH'S ARK: WHAT YOU DON'T NOAH

HERE ARE TWO WORDS I'm sure you've heard before: *Noah's ark*.

According to the Bible, Noah's ark is a reality, and not just a bunch of bull, or even bulls. But when you think about the story, what comes to mind? A drunk fellow named Noah? Animals grouped by fourteen climbing aboard a big boat? A ship landing on a mountain other than Mount Ararat?

Sorry if none of this immediately rings a bell. I'm just referring to what's actually in the Bible, and not what most people assume it says.

Today's world is simply drowning in misconceptions about the famous, ancient Flood. It's time to toss everything you thought you knew overboard, and finally learn "what you don't Noah."

When Old Meant Ancient

According to Genesis, Noah lived in a time when people enjoyed very long life spans. Noah's recorded story, in fact, picks up when he was already half a millennium old: "And Noah was five hundred years old: and Noah begat Shem, Ham, and Japheth" (5:32).

The few things Scripture reveals about Noah indicate that he was a rare good guy living in a very nasty time:

And God saw that the wickedness of man was great in the earth, and that every imagination of the thoughts of his heart was only evil continually.

99

And it repented the LORD that he had made man on the earth, and it grieved him at his heart. And the LORD said, I will destroy man whom I have created from the face of the earth; both man, and beast, and the creeping thing, and the fowls of the air; for it repenteth me that I have made them. But Noah found grace in the eyes of the LORD. These are the generations of Noah: Noah was a just man and perfect in his generations, and Noah walked with God. (6:5–9)

God grew so fed up with corruption that He decided to wipe the world clean of virtually all inhabitants and start over with Noah and his immediate family. God instructed Noah to build a giant ark to carry them through the coming Flood:

And God said unto Noah, The end of all flesh is come before me; for the earth is filled with violence through them; and, behold, I will destroy them with the earth. Make thee an ark of gopher wood; rooms shalt thou make in the ark, and shalt pitch it within and without with pitch. (vv. 13–14)

The phrase "gopher wood" has intrigued scholars for centuries, as no one is really sure exactly what it means. The local hardware story certainly doesn't carry gopher wood. Some think it disappeared during the Flood. Others suggest it could be any of a number of typical woods today, such as cypress, cedar, pine, acacia, juniper, ebony, or fir. Some claim it's a method of processing wood to make it more durable. Still others think it was not a wood at all, but reeds covered in cement. Whatever the ark was made from, the Bible shows that Noah obediently constructed the vessel and loaded it up with animals.

Counting Crows

This brings us to what is perhaps the most prevalent misconception about the story.

Many assume that there were two of every kind of animal brought aboard the boat, a male and female of each animal variety. People often see artwork featuring two cattle, two sheep, two goats, two deer, two buffalo, a rooster and hen, etc. They get this idea from the following verses of God's direct instruction to Noah:

And of every living thing of all flesh, two of every sort shalt thou bring into the ark, to keep them alive with thee; they shall be male and female. Of fowls after their kind, and of cattle after their kind, of every creeping thing of the earth after his kind, two of every sort shall come unto thee, to keep them alive. (vv. 19–20)

Unfortunately, most people do not read the rest of the story, which proves that not just two of every animal boarded Noah's ark. There were more—many more. To be precise, there were fourteen cattle, fourteen sheep, fourteen deer, fourteen buffalo, and seven roosters and seven hens.

The portion of the Genesis story many miss is that while two of each kind of unclean animal, like an elephant or a hippopotamus, sailed, Noah also spared seven pairs of each clean animal, those fit for eating, according to God. Thus, seven males and seven females of each kind of clean animal came aboard, for a total of fourteen:

And the LORD said unto Noah, Come thou and all thy house into the ark; for thee have I seen righteous before me in this generation. Of every clean beast thou shalt take to thee by sevens, the male and his female: and of beasts that are not clean by two, the male and his female. Of fowls also of the air by sevens, the male and the female; to keep seed alive upon the face of all the earth. (7:1–3)

A few verses later it mentions that the animals entered the ark two by two, one pair at a time, whether they were clean or unclean: "Of clean beasts, and of beasts that are not clean, and of fowls, and of every thing that creepeth upon the earth, there went in two and two unto Noah into the ark, the male and the female, as God had commanded Noah" (vv. 8–9).

A complete list of which animals are clean and unclean is provided in the eleventh chapter of the book of Leviticus, but it's apparent that righteous Noah was acquainted with God's dietary laws and followed the directions.

Additionally, people get it wrong when they assume Noah and his family were aboard the ark for only forty days. They remember a verse that states, "And the rain was upon the earth forty days and forty nights" (v. 12).

But it took months for the waters to vanish.

From start to finish, more than a year went by from when the rain started to when Noah was finally able to disembark: "In the six hundredth year of Noah's life, in the second month, the seventeenth day of the month, the same day were all the fountains of the great deep broken up, and the windows of heaven were opened" (v. 11).

As we see, Noah was six hundred years old when the waters began flowing on the seventeenth day of the second month. But it took many months before the waters dried and Noah left the boat.

> And it came to pass in the six hundredth and first year, in the first month, the first day of the month, the waters were dried up from off the earth: and Noah removed the covering of the ark, and looked, and, behold, the face of the ground was dry. And in the second month, on the seven and twentieth day of the month, was the earth dried. And God spake unto Noah, saying, Go forth of the ark, thou, and thy wife, and thy sons, and thy sons' wives with thee. (8:13–16)

The disembarking was clearly more than a year after the rain began. Noah was now 601, and God told him on the twenty-seventh day of the second month to leave the vessel.

The Landing Strip

As for the ark's final resting place, many people assume the boat landed upon what is known today as Mount Ararat in the modern nation of Turkey. But the Bible is not that precise. Here is what it does say in a variety of translations, in Genesis 8:4:

> And the ark rested in the seventh month, on the seventeenth day of the month, upon the mountains of Ararat. (KJV)

> Exactly five months from the time the flood began, the boat came to rest on the mountains of Ararat. (NLT)

> And on the seventeenth day of the seventh month the ark came to rest on the mountains of Ararat. (NIV)

The Scripture is consistent throughout translations that the vessel landed in the mountains (plural) of Ararat, not the mountain (singular) of Ararat.

And there is no guarantee that the Ararat named in Scripture is even the same Ararat in Turkey today. Searches for the legendary ark continue, and some maintain that a boat-shaped object on a mountain a few miles away from Ararat are the remains of the ship. One travel agency has even marketed Noah's ark tours to the site near Dogubayazit, Turkey.

While the story of the Flood seems incredible, Jesus Christ Himself mentioned Noah, the ark, and the Flood as facts, rather than as a bedtime fable: "In those days before the flood, the people enjoyed banquets and parties and weddings right up to the time Noah entered his boat and the flood came to destroy them all" (Luke 17:27 NLT).

Noah was certainly sober enough to remember the events of the Flood accurately. But he didn't always stay that way. The Bible indicates that Noah got drunk at some point after the Flood was over and he was back on solid ground. "And Noah began to be a husbandman, and he planted a vineyard: and he drank of the wine, and was drunken" (Genesis 9:20–21).

Explaining one element of the biblical record would be much easier if Noah and everyone else were drunk. But that isn't an option. While it is an incredible tale, it's rarely repeated in churches:

> And it came to pass, when men began to multiply on the face of the earth, and daughters were born unto them, that the sons of God saw the daughters of men that they were fair; and they took them wives of all which they chose. And the LORD said, My spirit shall not always strive with man, for that he also is flesh: yet his days shall be an hundred and twenty years. There were giants in the earth in those days; and also after that, when the sons of God came in unto the daughters of men, and they bare children to them, the same became mighty men which were of old, men of renown. (6:1–4)

Giants? Yes, giants are mentioned in the Bible, but there are different theories about what the Bible means. Some believe the Bible means precisely what it says, that there were indeed literal, physical giants. After all, the word *giants* occurs thirteen times in eleven verses of the King James Version, and usually indicates large people.

In another verse containing the same word *giants*, translated from the same Hebrew word *nephilim*, a band of Hebrew spies said, "And there we saw the giants, the sons of Anak, which come of the giants: and we were in our own sight as grasshoppers, and so we were in their sight" (Numbers 13:33).

One popular Flood theory claims these giants were the hybrid offspring of rebellious angels and human women, as the Bible says, "The sons of God came in unto the daughters of men, and they bare children to them, the same became mighty men which were of old, men of renown."

But others argue that this account has nothing to with angels having sex with humans. They believe the phrase "sons of God" refers to men who were faithful to God, and the "daughters of men" refers to pagan women. Their offspring were famous people, the "giants" of their day, as Steven Spielberg, Mel Gibson, and Donald Trump might be considered in ours. The verses have prompted endless speculation, but the Bible simply does not make clear exactly what it's referring to when it speaks of "giants."

The fact of the matter, though, is that the giants are mentioned in the midst of the story of Noah. They appear just prior to God's edict that He is going to flood the Earth and use Noah to repopulate it. This has prompted Bible readers to think about the circumstances that led to the Flood. Remember, we have read, "And God saw that the wickedness of man was great in the earth, and that every imagination of the thoughts of his heart was only evil continually" (Genesis 6:5).

While we are not given specifics, the very placement of the giants during a time of astounding wickedness immediately before the Flood of Noah has led many to suggest that the giants themselves had something to do with the reason the entire population of the planet was destroyed by God. If they indeed were the hybrid offspring of angels mating with human women, then perhaps God saw the need to purge Earth of something that was not part of the original creation. But it is not clearly spelled out in the pages of Scripture.

Now that you're no longer floundering in all the fish tales about Noah and his ark, you might be interested in what the Bible says about all those animals he was carrying. It may even change your mind about what you have for dinner tonight.

CHAPTER THIRTEEN

DOG FOR DINNER?

AN OLD JOKE asks, "What's the difference between a pig and a fox?"

The answer? "Three drinks."

If you chuckled at that, you've probably spent time in a bar, as people's perception changes as more alcohol is consumed. All kidding aside, the Bible suggests that when it comes to a suitable dinner, a pig and a fox are equally revolting to God. Food is a sensitive subject for many, but you might be thrown for a loop when you learn what the Bible says about the items so many people take for granted.

The Bible has much to say about what foods God finds acceptable for human consumption. Some very popular items—including what millions of Americans eat every day for breakfast, lunch, and dinner—are considered by the Creator of the universe to be inedible. If you think eating a dog, for example, is disgusting, you will be happy to know that God agrees with you. Of course, God expressed the same opinion about pork and shellfish.

Now, before I continue, I wish to state unequivocally that I am not the food police. It's none of my business what people choose to eat, whether or not it's good for them. But I am going to show you where you can find in Scripture what God says about certain foods and offer some ideas for discussion.

Going back to the very beginning, God told human beings in Genesis, "And God said, Behold, I have given you every herb bearing seed, which is upon the face of all the earth, and every tree, in which is the fruit of a tree yielding seed; to you it shall be for meat" (1:29).

With *meat* being the old English term for food, the verse seems self-explanatory.

The first dietary restriction found in Scripture is one that people today probably rarely think about. It was so important that its violation led to mankind's downfall. God told Adam and Eve that they could eat from any tree found in the garden of Eden, with the exception of one—the tree of the knowledge of good and evil: "And the LORD God commanded the man, saying, Of every tree of the garden thou mayest freely eat: But of the tree of the knowledge of good and evil, thou shalt not eat of it: for in the day that thou eatest thereof thou shalt surely die" (Genesis 2:16–17).

People who think God has no interest in our diet forget that the first test of obedience He gave Adam and Eve involved their daily diet.

Of course, Adam and Eve disobeyed God's command and ate the forbidden fruit. This ancient rebellion provides a clue as to why so many people in our modern day do not even consider what God says about diet. Just as mankind did not follow God's food instructions thousands of years ago, people today continue to decide for themselves what is appropriate. It's a lasting echo from the first diet ever created.

The Menu of God

God placed foods in two categories for humans: clean and unclean. As the words imply, clean foods are suitable for eating, and unclean foods are not. While Leviticus 11 contains the initial list, it's not the first place in Scripture that mentions clean and unclean foods. In Genesis, just before God flooded the Earth, He instructed Noah to build an ark and load it with many animals. God told Noah to gather a male and female of each of the unclean animals, but seven pairs of each of the clean animals (7:2).

We have no indication that Noah did not know what God meant. Noah apparently knew the difference between clean and unclean animals. Thus, he did as the Lord instructed him, and gathered seven pairs of clean animals (cattle, goat, sheep, etc.). He and his family were going to be aboard the ark for a long time—a lot longer than forty days—and they needed a good supply of food.

When the ark finally came to rest on dry ground, Scripture indicates that Noah sacrificed some of the clean animals: "And Noah builded an altar unto the LORD; and took of every clean beast, and of every clean fowl, and offered burnt offerings on the altar" (Genesis 8:20).

Some claim that the sole purpose for which Noah brought aboard so many more clean animals than unclean was for sacrificing once they left the vessel. Sacrificing, however, did not mean flame broiling an animal and then throwing the meat away. While a burnt offering usually was not consumed, most sacrifices were meant to be eaten. So it's highly likely that Noah and his family enjoyed prime rib, mutton, and venison in addition to completely burning some of the sacrificed animals.

Thus, we see from Noah's experience that the food laws mentioned in Leviticus were already in force back in the time recorded in Genesis. God did not suddenly write these laws in Leviticus; the guidelines already existed.

God sometimes spelled out the difference between clean and unclean by naming the precise creature, or at least specifying certain characteristics that allowed humans to know whether or not an animal was permissible to consume. This information comes in handy when dealing with the large variety of sea creatures. There are many kinds of different seafood, but there is just one phrase to keep in mind when trying to determine what God named as permissible to eat: "fins and scales."

These shall ye eat of all that are in the waters: whatsoever hath fins and scales in the waters, in the seas, and in the rivers, them shall ye eat. And all that have not fins and scales in the seas, and in the rivers, of all that move in the waters, and of any living thing which is in the waters, they shall be an abomination unto you: They shall be even an abomination unto you; ye shall not eat of their flesh, but ye shall have their carcases in abomination. Whatsoever hath no fins nor scales in the waters, that shall be an abomination unto you. (Leviticus 11:9–12)

God made it clear that if a sea creature does not have fins and scales, it should not be on the menu. Popular foods that *don't* have fins and scales include catfish, clams, crabs, lobsters, mussels, oysters, scallops, shark, shrimp, squid, and swordfish.

Shellfish enthusiasts might be disappointed at reading this. But think about this for a moment. Shellfish, such as crabs and lobsters, are bottom-feeding scavengers. They survive off diseased and dead creatures that fall to the bottom of the sea. Shellfish such as clams, mussels, and shrimp dwell in their own waste. Perhaps the associated bacteria are not meant to interact with the human body, and that's why God called eating these sea critters an "abomination"—the same word He used to describe homosexuality.

Some popular fish that are clean and fit for eating according to the Bible include albacore, bass, barracuda, cod, herring, flounder, haddock, halibut, mackerel, mahi mahi (also known as dolphin fish, but not to be confused with the mammal dolphin, which is unclean), perch, pike, pompano, salmon, sardines, snapper, snook, tarpon, trout, tuna, and whitefish.

Land Ho!

When it comes to land animals, the determining factors are obviously not "fins and scales." Instead, think foot and mouth. Anything with a paw is not clean. As for the rest, here is what the Bible says:

> Whatsoever parteth the hoof, and is clovenfooted, and cheweth the cud, among the beasts, that shall ye eat. Nevertheless these shall ye not eat of them that chew the cud, or of them that divide the hoof: as the camel, because he cheweth the cud, but divideth not the hoof; he is unclean unto you. And the coney, because he cheweth the cud, but divideth not the hoof; he is unclean unto you. And the hare, because he cheweth the cud, but divideth not the hoof; he is unclean unto you. And the swine, though he divide the hoof, and be clovenfooted, yet he cheweth not the cud; he is unclean to you. Of their flesh shall ye not eat, and their carcase shall ye not touch; they are unclean to you. (Leviticus 11:3–8)

For those who don't know what "chew the cud" means, it's simply rechewing food that was chewed and swallowed previously. Some animals, such as cattle, have more than one stomach, and their digestive process involves partially chewing food and swallowing it into one stomach. They then regurgitate it to chew again before swallowing it again into another stomach.

Since cattle have cloven, or "split," hooves, and they ruminate (chew the cud), they are clean for eating. So don't feel guilty about ordering the porterhouse steak next time you have a night on the town. And while most people in the Western Hemisphere are not big camel eaters, millions of Westerners savor the meat from pigs, despite the prohibition by God. Remember, this is not the Islamic Koran we're reading from. It is the Holy Bible. Eating pig meat is in the same category as eating rat or gorilla.

I have heard the question many times, "Why did God create pigs, if not for people to eat them?"

To that I respond, "Why did God create skunks and monkeys?" The response is not meant to be flippant; God created many things not meant for human consumption.

God created poisonous natural gases and natural toxic substances found in plants such as rosary pea, castor bean, and foxglove. Eating them can kill humans. Just because God has created something does not mean He intended human beings to ingest it.

Clean land animals include not only popular food choices such as cattle and sheep but also buffalo, goat, deer, elk, moose, and even giraffe.

The list of unclean animals is much longer than the clean list and includes armadillo, badger, bear, beaver, camel, cat, cheetah, coyote, dog, donkey, elephant, ferret, fox, gorilla, groundhog, hippopotamus, horse, hyena, jackal, kangaroo, leopard, lion, llama, mole, monkey, mouse, mule, muskrat, opossum, panther, pig (hog, bacon, ham, lard, pork), porcupine, rabbit, raccoon, rat, rhinoceros, skunk, slug, snail, squirrel, tiger, wallaby, weasel, wolf, wolverine, worm, and zebra.

In addition, all reptiles and amphibians are considered unclean. This includes alligator, crocodile, frog, lizard, newt, salamander, snake, toad, and turtle.

Crying Fowl

Fans of Southern fried chicken or Thanksgiving Day turkey have no need to worry, because both chicken and turkey are considered clean birds. But just because others may "taste like chicken," as some supposedly do, does not make them suitable for humans to eat.

Other clean birds include duck, goose, pheasant, and quail.

The list of unclean fowl is found in Leviticus 11:13–19 and includes eagles, herons, ospreys, owls, pelicans, storks, and vultures, among others.

For people interested in eating insects, you'll be happy to know that the leaping kind, such as crickets, grasshoppers, and locusts, are all considered clean and permissible to eat. Those familiar with the New Testament will likely recall that John the Baptist was known for eating "locusts and wild honey" (Matthew 3:4).

New Diet Same as the Old Diet?

It is clear which foods the Bible labels as clean and unclean, but was there ever a change in the status of these foods? I realize most people, including the vast majority of Christians, believe it's permissible to eat anything. But let's take a look at some verses that relate to the question.

One of the most often cited sections is in Mark's gospel, where some suggest Jesus Christ came right out and made some kind of declaration that all foods are now clean.

> And he saith unto them, Are ye so without understanding also? Do ye not perceive, that whatsoever thing from without entereth into the man, it cannot defile him; because it entereth not into his heart, but into the belly, and goeth out into the draught, purging all meats? (7:18–19)

The verses do not say Jesus declared all meats clean. Even in the original Greek, those words simply are not there. The text should be examined in its context to get the full meaning of what Jesus says. The chapter starts out by specifically talking about eating without first washing one's hands: "Then the Pharisees and scribes asked him, Why walk not thy disciples according to the tradition of the elders, but eat bread with unwashen hands?" (v. 5).

Jesus responded by blasting those who put forth such a question, saying they were more interested in following some man-made tradition than the laws of God.

> Howbeit in vain do they worship me, teaching for doctrines the commandments of men. For laying aside the commandment of God, ye hold the tradition of men, as the washing of pots and cups: and many other such like things ye do. And he said unto them, Full well ye reject the commandment of God, that ye may keep your own tradition. (vv. 7–9)

Notice, the subject at hand has nothing to do with clean or unclean foods. He then made this statement: "There is nothing from without a man, that entering into him can defile him: but the things which come out of him, those are they that defile the man" (v. 15).

His disciples did not understand what he was talking about, and Jesus explained the meaning to them, as recorded in the subsequent verses.

And when he was entered into the house from the people, his disciples asked him concerning the parable. And he saith unto them, Are ye so without understanding also? Do ye not perceive, that whatsoever thing from without entereth into the man, it cannot defile him; because it entereth not into his heart, but into the belly, and goeth out into the draught, purging all meats? And he said, That which cometh out of the man, that defileth the man. For from within, out of the heart of men, proceed evil thoughts, adulteries, fornications, murders, thefts, covetousness, wickedness, deceit, lasciviousness, an evil eye, blasphemy, pride, foolishness: All these evil things come from within, and defile the man. (vv. 17–23)

Again, we find no thunderous pronouncement from Jesus that instantaneously changed the nature of unclean foods to clean. The subject at hand is washing before a meal. Jesus explained that if something like a speck of dirt went into someone's mouth, it would be purged out in that person's digestive system. He was much more concerned with what was inside the minds and hearts of people, as he listed numerous "evil thoughts" and bad attitudes that defile people.

Vision Quest

Another section often cited about food is the tenth chapter of Acts, which tells of the apostle Peter receiving an interesting vision:

Peter went up upon the housetop to pray about the sixth hour: And he became very hungry, and would have eaten: but while they made ready, he fell into a trance, and saw heaven opened, and a certain vessel descending unto him, as it had been a great sheet knit at the four corners, and let down to the earth: wherein were all manner of fourfooted beasts of the earth, and wild beasts, and creeping things, and fowls of the air. And there came a voice to him, Rise, Peter; kill, and eat. But Peter said, Not so, Lord; for I have never eaten any thing that is common or unclean. And the voice spake unto him again the second time, What God hath cleansed, that call not thou common. This was done thrice: and the vessel was received up again into heaven. (vv. 9–16)

In his vision, Peter saw a number of unclean animals, and was told to kill them and eat them. People who feel it's now perfectly fine to eat any kind of creature often cite these verses, believing all unclean foods have been made fit to eat.

But examine it closely, because the story continues. This incident took place years after the death and resurrection of Jesus. Peter himself stated that he had never eaten anything unclean. This is further proof that Jesus, during His ministry, never declared all foods to be clean. If He had done so, then Peter, a devout disciple, would have been eating them. But as mentioned before, Jesus did not declare all foods to be clean, and therefore Peter correctly abstained from them.

Secondly, Peter did not take this vision to mean that God was making unclean foods clean. At first, he did not even understand what his vision meant.

Now while Peter doubted in himself what this vision which he had seen should mean, behold, the men which were sent from Cornelius had made enquiry for Simon's house, and stood before the gate, and called, and asked whether Simon, which was surnamed Peter, were lodged there. While Peter thought on the vision, the Spirit said unto him, Behold, three men seek thee. (vv. 17–19)

Peter found three men, all of whom were not Jews, seeking him. They were pagans, Gentiles, all considered to be "unclean" people by Jews, and therefore not suitable for contact with them. That is when the meaning of the vision finally hit Peter, and it had nothing to do with animals or food.

And he said unto them, Ye know how that it is an unlawful thing for a man that is a Jew to keep company, or come unto one of another nation; but God hath shewed me that I should not call any man common or unclean . . . Then Peter opened his mouth, and said, Of a truth I perceive that God is no respecter of persons: But in every nation he that feareth him, and worketh righteousness, is accepted with him. (vv. 28, 34–35)

God was telling Peter that no *human being* is to be considered unclean. People of any race, ethnicity, or country are accepted by God. The Jews who had become Christians were quite stunned when they learned of this acceptance and saw Gentiles filled with the power of God.

The Jewish believers who came with Peter were amazed that the gift of the Holy Spirit had been poured out upon the Gentiles, too. And there could be no doubt about it, for they heard them speaking in tongues and praising God. Then Peter asked, "Can anyone object to their being baptized, now that they have received the Holy Spirit just as we did?" (vv. 45–47 NLT)

Doctrines of Devils

Yet another portion of Scripture that some believe implies that anything is now permissible to eat is 1 Timothy 4:1–5:

Now the Spirit speaketh expressly, that in the latter times some shall depart from the faith, giving heed to seducing spirits, and doctrines of devils; Speaking lies in hypocrisy; having their conscience seared with a hot iron; forbidding to marry, and commanding to abstain from meats, which God hath created to be received with thanksgiving of them which believe and know the truth. For every creature of God is good, and nothing to be refused, if it be received with thanksgiving: For it is sanctified by the word of God and prayer.

Among the supposed doctrines of devils is the command to abstain from meats. Does this mean the exclusion of unclean meats from one's diet is a doctrine of devils? Hardly. Remember, God Himself gave explicit instructions to abstain from certain meats.

The apostle Paul warned in his letter to Timothy that in the latter days people would adhere to ridiculous beliefs, one of which was abstaining from all meats—in other words, vegetarianism. The New Age movement is one of the powerful forces behind the trend of eating only fruits and vegetables.

And despite some billboards you might see from People for the Ethical Treatment of Animals, Jesus Himself was not a vegetarian. He ate plenty of animal meat during His life, especially during Passover, when it was commanded that a lamb be slain for the holiday meal: "Now the Festival of Unleavened Bread arrived, when the Passover lambs were sacrificed. Jesus sent Peter and John ahead and said, 'Go and prepare the Passover meal, so we can eat it together'" (Luke 22:7–8 NLT).

But some argue that everything is permissible to eat, since Paul wrote, "For every creature of God is good, and nothing to be refused, if it be received with thanksgiving" (1 Timothy 4:4). They often fail to mention the next verse, which clarifies the meaning: "For it is sanctified by the word of God and prayer" (v. 5).

Paul and Timothy had only the Old Testament as their Scripture, since the New Testament had not yet been written. The foods approved for eating in the Old Testament appear in Leviticus 11 and Deuteronomy 14. Eating puppy dogs, monkeys, and worms does not suddenly become permissible if a prayer is uttered. The foods still have to be set apart, sanctified by the laws of God.

While some suggest Jesus did away with Old Testament laws, He Himself said the exact opposite, stressing that He came to show everyone how to obey God's law to its fullest extent:

> Think not that I am come to destroy the law, or the prophets: I am not come to destroy, but to fulfil. For verily I say unto you, Till heaven and earth pass, one jot or one tittle shall in no wise pass from the law, till all be fulfilled. Whosoever therefore shall break one of these least commandments, and shall teach men so, he shall be called the least in the kingdom of heaven: but whosoever shall do and teach them, the same shall be called great in the kingdom of heaven. (Matthew 5:17–19)

Even in the future, when Jesus will come back to Earth at His "second coming," people who eat unclean foods are going to have a problem, at least according to the book of Isaiah. The prophet foresaw the end times and noted that God would slay many people at that time. He even made special mention that people eating "abominations" such as pig meat and mice will be in trouble, to say the least.

For, behold, the LORD will come with fire, and with his chariots like a whirlwind, to render his anger with fury, and his rebuke with flames of fire. For by fire and by his sword will the LORD plead with all flesh: and the slain of the LORD shall be many. They that sanctify themselves, and purify themselves in the gardens behind one tree in the midst, eating swine's flesh, and the abomination, and the mouse, shall be consumed together, saith the LORD. (66:15-17)

If Jesus had at some point declared all foods clean, Isaiah's prophecy means nothing and merits no place in the Holy Bible.

The idea that some foods are clean and others are unclean is present in the whole Bible, not just the Old Testament. God cares about what we put into our mouths, not because He doesn't want us to enjoy His creation, but because He wants us to enjoy it rightly. And as most Christians have never thought about their diet, it's stunning to hear that the Bible speaks with one voice on the issue.

CHAPTER FOURTEEN

YOUR WISH IS MY COMMANDMENT

EVERYONE HAS LIKELY heard of Moses and the Ten Commandments, but have you ever heard about twenty commandments?

Did you know Moses spent eighty days without anything to eat or drink while waiting for the commandments to be ready? And did you know people were so afraid of what Moses looked like after he received the laws that he had to have his head "bagged"?

If thou continuest reading, thou shalt learn the Bible truth about the Ten Commandments.

Ten Commandments . . . or Is That Twenty?

The first point concerns the actual number of commandments. Is it just ten, or twice that number?

Actually, both are true. Here's the explanation. There are indeed ten main instructions from God. They're even referred to three times in the Old Testament precisely as the "ten commandments."

> And he wrote upon the tables the words of the covenant, the ten commandments. (Exodus 34:28)

> And he declared unto you his covenant, which he commanded you to perform, even ten commandments. (Deuteronomy 4:13)

And he wrote on the tables, according to the first writing, the ten commandments, which the LORD spake unto you in the mount out of the midst of the fire in the day of the assembly: and the LORD gave them unto me. (Deuteronomy 10:4)

However, when the original set was inscribed on two stone tablets, an enraged Moses smashed the laws when he came down from Mount Sinai. He discovered that God's chosen people were engaged in sinful activity, including the worship of a golden calf idol. "And it came to pass, as soon as he came nigh unto the camp, that he saw the calf, and the dancing: and Moses' anger waxed hot, and he cast the tables out of his hands, and brake them beneath the mount" (Exodus 32:19).

With the original pair smashed to pieces, a second set of the same laws was subsequently inscribed, thus bringing the total number to twenty. Many have either forgotten or simply remain unaware that the famous Ten Commandments had to be reproduced from scratch: "And the LORD said unto Moses, Hew thee two tables of stone like unto the first: and I will write upon these tables the words that were in the first tables, which thou brakest" (Exodus 34:1).

So, the Ten Commandments were actually written twice, for a grand total of twenty.

Here are a few interesting notes about them:

First, despite novelty replicas sold in stores today depicting the writing solely on one side, the Ten Commandments were actually inscribed on both the front and back of the stone tablets: "The tables were written on both their sides; on the one side and on the other were they written" (Exodus 32:15).

Also, while Moses was responsible for cutting out the tablets to use for the laws, he himself did not write the commandments. They were inscribed by God, engraved by God's own finger. This fact is mentioned in at least two verses, with no comment about the penmanship.

And he gave unto Moses, when he had made an end of communing with him upon mount Sinai, two tables of testimony, tables of stone, written with the finger of God. (Exodus 31:18)

And the tables were the work of God, and the writing was the writing of God, graven upon the tables. (Exodus 32:16)

And finally, lest we overlook the obvious, the Ten Commandments were written in the Hebrew language, not the English of 1611, so there's not a single "Thou shalt not" on the original tablets. All translations today just make their best attempt to convey the meaning.

In case you've never seen them before, here is their first listing in Scripture, located in the twentieth chapter of Exodus:

> I am the LORD thy God, which have brought thee out of the land of Egypt, out of the house of bondage. Thou shalt have no other gods before me. Thou shalt not make unto thee any graven image, or any likeness of any thing that is in heaven above, or that is in the earth beneath, or that is in the water under the earth: Thou shalt not bow down thyself to them, nor serve them: for I the LORD thy God am a jealous God, visiting the iniquity of the fathers upon the children unto the third and fourth generation of them that hate me; and shewing mercy unto thousands of them that love me, and keep my commandments. Thou shalt not take the name of the LORD thy God in vain; for the LORD will not hold him guiltless that taketh his name in vain. Remember the sabbath day, to keep it holy. Six days shalt thou labour, and do all thy work: But the seventh day is the sabbath of the LORD thy God: in it thou shalt not do any work, thou, nor thy son, nor thy daughter, thy manservant, nor thy maidservant, nor thy cattle, nor thy stranger that is within thy gates: For in six days the LORD made heaven and earth, the sea, and all that in them is, and rested the seventh day: wherefore the LORD blessed the sabbath day, and hallowed it. Honour thy father and thy mother: that thy days may be long upon the land which the LORD thy God giveth thee. Thou shalt not kill. Thou shalt not commit adultery. Thou shalt not steal. Thou shalt not bear false witness against thy neighbour. Thou shalt not covet thy neighbour's house, thou shalt not covet thy neighbour's wife, nor his manservant, nor his maidservant, nor his ox, nor his ass, nor any thing that is thy neighbour's. (vv. 2–17)

Hunger for Justice

Though it may seem impossible, Moses had no food or drink for eighty days while he waited for God to give him the holy laws—almost three complete months without nourishment. Not only that, but in the middle of that period, he climbed up a mountain.

Some may have thought Moses fasted for just forty days (as if forty were some small feat), but many are unaware that he immediately went on another forty-day stint without eating or drinking.

> When I was gone up into the mount to receive the tables of stone, even the tables of the covenant which the LORD made with you, then I abode in the mount forty days and forty nights, I neither did eat bread nor drink water: And the LORD delivered unto me two tables of stone written with the finger of God; and on them was written according to all the words, which the LORD spake with you in the mount out of the midst of the fire in the day of the assembly. And it came to pass at the end of forty days and forty nights, that the LORD gave me the two tables of stone, even the tables of the covenant. (Deuteronomy 9:9–11)

Moses came down the mountain and discovered his people, who had just been freed from Egyptian slavery, engaging in sin. He smashed the tablets to pieces in his anger.

> And the LORD said unto me, Arise, get thee down quickly from hence; for thy people which thou hast brought forth out of Egypt have corrupted themselves; they are quickly turned aside out of the way which I commanded them; they have made them a molten image. (v. 12)

The passage records no indication that Moses ate as he descended the mountain.

> So I turned and came down from the mount, and the mount burned with fire: and the two tables of the covenant were in my two hands. And I looked, and, behold, ye had sinned against the LORD your God, and had made you a molten calf: ye had turned aside quickly out of the way which the LORD had commanded you. And I took the two tables, and cast them out of my two hands, and brake them before your eyes. And I fell down before the LORD, as at the first, forty days and forty nights: I did neither eat bread, nor drink water, because of all your sins which ye sinned, in doing wickedly in the sight of the LORD, to provoke him to anger. (vv. 15–18)

The New Living Translation makes it clear that Moses repeated the forty-day period without nourishment: "Then for forty days and nights I lay prostrate before the LORD, neither eating bread nor drinking water. I did this because you had sinned by doing what the LORD hated, thus making him very angry" (v. 18).

The book of Exodus confirms the second forty-day period of complete fasting. "And he was there with the LORD forty days and forty nights; he did neither eat bread, nor drink water. And he wrote upon the tables the words of the covenant, the ten commandments" (34:28).

While two separate forty-day fasts clearly occurred, it's not clear if Moses ate or drank anything during the time periods between his coming down the mountain and smashing the first set of tablets, and his climb to receive the second pair.

More information about the timeline can be found in chapters 32 through 34 of Exodus. After Moses' initial descent from Mount Sinai, he ordered the execution of some three thousand fellow Israelites who did not respond to his call (Exodus 32:25–28). Moses made this proclamation the following day: "Ye have sinned a great sin: and now I will go up unto the LORD; peradventure I shall make an atonement for your sin" (v. 30).

Moses spent at least one day in the camp. Moreover, one additional day may have passed before he began his return trip, as chapter 34 commences with this command from God:

> Hew thee two tables of stone like unto the first: and I will write upon these tables the words that were in the first tables, which thou brakest. And be ready in the morning, and come up in the morning unto mount Sinai, and present thyself there to me in the top of the mount. And no man shall come up with thee, neither let any man be seen throughout all the mount; neither let the flocks nor herds feed before that mount. And he hewed two tables of stone like unto the first; and Moses rose up early in the morning, and went up unto mount Sinai, as the LORD had commanded him, and took in his hand the two tables of stone. And the LORD descended in the cloud, and stood with him there, and proclaimed the name of the LORD. (vv. 1–5)

God told Moses to "be ready in the morning, and come up in the morning." Moses apparently spent at least one night, and perhaps two, among his people in the camp before commencing his return hike. It's possible he ate and drank while in the camp, but the Bible is not absolutely clear on that point.

Remember, Moses made this statement regarding the creation of the first set of commandments: "And I took the two tables, and cast them out of my two hands, and brake them before your eyes. And I fell down before the LORD, as at the first, forty days and forty nights: I did neither eat bread, nor drink water" (Deuteronomy 9:17–18).

That leaves open the stunning possibility that Moses went without food and water for eighty consecutive days. Even if he ate between forty-day fasts, that's still eighty days out of eighty-one or eighty-two without nourishment.

Only two other biblical characters are known to have completed forty-day fasts. The prophet Elijah avoided food and water during a long journey cited in 1 Kings 19:7–8:

> And the angel of the LORD came again the second time, and touched him, and said, Arise and eat; because the journey is too great for thee. And he arose, and did eat and drink, and went in the strength of that meat forty days and forty nights unto Horeb the mount of God.

The New Testament records that Jesus completed His own period of forty days without food, with a critical test from the devil immediately following: "Then Jesus was led out into the wilderness by the Holy Spirit to be tempted there by the Devil. For forty days and forty nights he ate nothing and became very hungry" (Matthew 4:1–2 NLT).

Only Moses, though, is noted to have completed eighty days without eating or drinking.

The Shining

"Brilliant! Dazzling! Sensational! A must-see!"

I'm not sure whether or not the reviews for the movie *The Ten Commandments* used these words, but the Bible indicates that a spectacular thing happened to Moses—that freaked out his fellow Israelites. And no, he was not selling pork chops at half price.

Moses' face blazed with an incredible brilliance after he received the second set of tablets containing the Ten Commandments. The glamorous event is first mentioned in the thirty-fourth chapter of Exodus.

When Moses came down the mountain carrying the stone tablets inscribed with the terms of the covenant, he wasn't aware that his face glowed because he had spoken to the LORD face to face. And when Aaron and the people of Israel saw the radiance of Moses' face, they were afraid to come near him. But Moses called to them and asked Aaron and the community leaders to come over and talk with him. (vv. 29–31 NLT)

Moses was obviously completely in the dark about his face brightening: the text says, "He wasn't aware that his face glowed." Only after Aaron and the rest of the Israelites caught a glimpse of Moses' shiny face did Moses realize that something had changed since the last time he saw his people. "Then all the people came, and Moses gave them the instructions the Lord had given him on Mount Sinai. When Moses had finished speaking with them, he put a veil over his face" (vv. 32–33 NLT).

God's servant Moses, who had led the Israelites out of Egypt with a series of miracles, now sported a glowing face that actually emanated light! To keep the people from panicking, Moses did what any reasonable person would. He covered his head:

But whenever he went into the Tent of Meeting to speak with the Lord, he removed the veil until he came out again. Then he would give the people whatever instructions the Lord had given him, and the people would see his face aglow. Afterward he would put the veil on again until he returned to speak with the Lord. (vv. 34–35 NLT)

Moses' face was so brilliant that he covered it with a veil when in the presence of others, and only took the veil off when he spoke with God, the obvious source of the glow. Ironically, over the course of decades, the Israelites grumbled about Moses, suggesting he did not have a special connection with God. As we're about to see, many of those malcontent Israelites paid with their lives for remaining in the dark.

CHAPTER FIFTEEN

THE BIGGEST KILLER IN THE BIBLE

I'VE KILLED MORE MEN than Cecil B. DeMille."

That famous punch line from the Mel Brooks comedy *Blazing Saddles* was delivered by Gene Wilder, who played a deadly gunslinger called the Waco Kid. DeMille, you recall, was the one who directed the movie *The Ten Commandments*, in which many die in the dramatization of the biblical story. Wilder's point was that many people get whacked in the Bible.

From start to finish, corpses seem to pile up everywhere in Scripture. Readers find numerous accounts of murder, execution, human sacrifice, war-related casualties, natural disasters such as famines and earthquakes, and the ever-popular "dropping dead."

But who is the biggest killer in the Bible? The fact is that it's God Himself.

Scripture states that God ordered capital punishment for men, women, and even young children—sometimes in very large numbers. It may disturb modern people (especially opponents of capital punishment), but thousands, perhaps millions, of human beings experienced death either by God's direct hand or His edict.

But first, a quick word of warning, as some of this may not be easy to read. Today, Christians and non-Christians alike are so inundated with messages about God's love and forgiveness that they have simply never learned about the vast number of people God has slain or the circumstances of their deaths. Discussing the issue can lead to some difficult questions about the real nature of God.

The Death Toll

The largest mass execution in world history occurred in the great Flood of Noah's time, recorded in Genesis. The entire global population—with the exception of Noah, his wife, and their three sons and their wives—drowned when God flooded the world with water.

> And every living substance was destroyed which was upon the face of the ground, both man, and cattle, and the creeping things, and the fowl of the heaven; and they were destroyed from the earth: and Noah only remained alive, and they that were with him in the ark. (7:23)

God spared only Noah's immediate family. Every other person, numbering perhaps into the millions, was killed by God. Even unborn children in the womb never got to see the light of day due to the deluge. The reason: "God saw that the wickedness of man was great in the earth, and that every imagination of the thoughts of his heart was only evil continually. And it repented the LORD that he had made man on the earth, and it grieved him at his heart" (Genesis 6:5–6).

Later, the residents of two ancient cities, found guilty of "very grievous" sin, suffered scorching deaths at the direct hand of God. "The LORD rained upon Sodom and upon Gomorrah brimstone and fire from the LORD out of heaven" (Genesis 19:24).

God also turned executioner during the time of the Exodus from Egypt—the Bible records that a massive plague snuffed out the lives of all the firstborn children of Egypt, while God spared the Israelites.

> And Moses said, Thus saith the LORD, About midnight will I go out into the midst of Egypt: And all the firstborn in the land of Egypt shall die, from the first born of Pharaoh that sitteth upon his throne, even unto the firstborn of the maidservant that is behind the mill; and all the firstborn of beasts. And there shall be a great cry throughout all the land of Egypt, such as there was none like it, nor shall be like it any more. But against

any of the children of Israel shall not a dog move his tongue, against man or beast: that ye may know how that the LORD doth put a difference between the Egyptians and Israel. (Exodus 11:4–7)

As if to stress the point that God Himself is the one acting as judge, jury, and executioner, the threat is repeated shortly thereafter: "For I will pass through the land of Egypt this night, and will smite all the firstborn in the land of Egypt, both man and beast; and against all the gods of Egypt I will execute judgment: I am the LORD" (12:12).

But God's wrath was not limited to pagans living in Egypt. Once His own people were freed from captivity, they quickly engaged in sinful behavior, creating an idol in the form of a golden calf. When Moses descended Mount Sinai and discovered the rebellious activity, he was ordered by God to execute those who chose not to be on the Lord's side—an estimated three thousand men.

And he said unto them, Thus saith the LORD God of Israel, Put every man his sword by his side, and go in and out from gate to gate throughout the camp, and slay every man his brother, and every man his companion, and every man his neighbour. And the children of Levi did according to the word of Moses: and there fell of the people that day about three thousand men. (Exodus 32:27–28)

During the Israelites' time in the wilderness and their takeover of the promised land, they received divine orders to kill men, women, children, and animals. We read in Numbers:

Og the king of Bashan went out against them, he, and all his people, to the battle at Edrei. And the LORD said unto Moses, Fear him not: for I have delivered him into thy hand, and all his people, and his land . . . So they smote him, and his sons, and all his people, until there was none left him alive: and they possessed his land. (21:33–35)

When Israelite men began having sex with the pagan Moabite women and adopted heathen practices such as bowing down and sacrificing to false gods, God became angry enough to slay some twenty-four thousand of His own people, most of whom were executed by hanging: "And the LORD said unto Moses, Take all the heads of the people, and hang them up before the LORD against the sun, that the fierce anger of the LORD may be turned away from Israel . . . And those that died in the plague were twenty and four thousand" (Numbers 25:4, 9).

When God exacted revenge against the Midianites who fought against His people, Moses was surprised to see women and children alive. So he ordered the slaughter of all nonvirgin women and male children: "Now therefore kill every male among the little ones, and kill every woman that hath known man by lying with him" (Numbers 31:17).

God ordered the destruction of Sihon and his descendants who fought against the Israelites. Note that even little children were not spared: "And we took all his cities at that time, and utterly destroyed the men, and the women, and the little ones, of every city, we left none to remain" (Deuteronomy 2:34).

God later explained that He did not want any pagan left alive to corrupt Israel. He would obviously not get the gold star from today's "tolerance" crowd.

> But of the cities of these people, which the LORD thy God doth give thee for an inheritance, thou shalt save alive nothing that breatheth: But thou shalt utterly destroy them; namely, the Hittites, and the Amorites, the Canaanites, and the Perizzites, the Hivites, and the Jebusites; as the LORD thy God hath commanded thee: that they teach you not to do after all their abominations, which they have done unto their gods; so should ye sin against the LORD your God. (Deuteronomy 20:16–18)

When the walls of ancient Jericho came crashing down at the blast of trumpets, Joshua and his men spared no one: "And they utterly destroyed all that was in the city, both man and woman, young and old, and ox, and sheep, and ass, with the edge of the sword" (Joshua 6:21).

Some twelve thousand were slain as God made Joshua's army victorious at a place called Ai:

> And it came to pass, when Israel had made an end of slaying all the inhabitants of Ai in the field, in the wilderness wherein they chased them, and when they were all fallen on the edge of the sword, until they were

consumed, that all the Israelites returned unto Ai, and smote it with the edge of the sword. And so it was, that all that fell that day, both of men and women, were twelve thousand, even all the men of Ai. (Joshua 8:24–25)

As Joshua's fighting men were killing enemies in battle, God Himself got involved, firing weapons from the sky and killing more people than did Joshua's army:

And it came to pass, as they fled from before Israel, and were in the going down to Bethhoron, that the LORD cast down great stones from heaven upon them unto Azekah, and they died: they were more which died with hailstones than they whom the children of Israel slew with the sword. (Joshua 10:11)

The point is made over and over again. God does get angry, and He kills men, women, and children, some of whom never even heard of Him. And His anger is not just an Old Testament phenomenon.

The Angry Passion of the Christ

Was Jesus Christ a hippie peacenik? Did he act like some ultra-laid-back California dude? Or was He low on testosterone? Apparently some folks in Hollywood think so. So many movies feature a soft-spoken, mild-mannered, almost effeminate Jesus sending a quiet, peaceful gaze toward heaven. Maybe the filmmakers think the Son of God acted differently from the God of the Old Testament, not realizing that Jesus is the same God of the Old Testament who carried out countless executions.

Unfortunately, the depictions of Jesus on film have led many to think Christ never got upset, angry, or violent. People think He was always calm and gentle. But Jesus was neither wimpy nor effeminate. In today's language, He would be considered a "tough guy" who had no qualms about showing the hotter side of His emotions.

The New Testament records Jesus verbally blasting His own disciples, calling other people harsh names, and making a public spectacle of Himself as he flailed around a whip and flipped over furniture that didn't belong to Him. This last incident is mentioned in all four of the Gospels, but the version in John contains the most information:

It was time for the annual Passover celebration, and Jesus went to Jerusalem. In the Temple area he saw merchants selling cattle, sheep, and doves for sacrifices; and he saw money changers behind their counters. Jesus made a whip from some ropes and chased them all out of the Temple. He drove out the sheep and oxen, scattered the money changers' coins over the floor, and turned over their tables. Then, going over to the people who sold doves, he told them, "Get these things out of here. Don't turn my Father's house into a marketplace!" (2:13–16 NLT)

What sparked this angry outburst? The holy temple in Jerusalem looked more like a flea market than a house of prayer. Jesus grew so angry at the desecration of His temple, He created His own scourge and whipped it around. He not only drove out the animals sold for sacrifices, He emptied the cash containers used by money exchangers before He overturned their tables.

According to the twenty-third chapter of Matthew, Jesus also used harsh names to emphasize His righteous anger. He was caustic with the religious leaders of His day, loudly labeling them hypocrites, blind guides, fools, snakes, and vipers. Jesus asked them in verse 33, "Ye serpents, ye generation of vipers, how can ye escape the damnation of hell?"

Even during times of miraculous healing, Jesus did not always remain calm and cool. Mark indicates that He was filled with anger as He restored a man's withered hand to complete health.

Jesus went into the synagogue again and noticed a man with a deformed hand. Since it was the Sabbath, Jesus' enemies watched him closely. Would he heal the man's hand on the Sabbath? If he did, they planned to condemn him. Jesus said to the man, "Come and stand in front of everyone." Then he turned to his critics and asked, "Is it legal to do good deeds on the Sabbath, or is it a day for doing harm? Is this a day to save life or to destroy it?" But they wouldn't answer him. He looked around at them angrily, because he was deeply disturbed by their hard hearts. Then he said to the man, "Reach out your hand." The man reached out his hand, and it became normal again! (3:1–5 NLT)

Jesus' own friends were not immune from His sharp reprimands. And according to Scripture, they were not afraid to rebuke Him either. A harsh exchange between Jesus and Peter came as Jesus predicted His own death and resurrection.

> But Peter took him aside and corrected him. "Heaven forbid, Lord," he said. "This will never happen to you!" Jesus turned to Peter and said, "Get away from me, Satan! You are a dangerous trap to me. You are seeing things merely from a human point of view, and not from God's." (Matthew 16:22–23 NLT)

Here, in no uncertain terms, while Peter was barking at Jesus, Jesus snapped back, calling Peter "Satan"—the name given to the devil. Surprisingly, this heated exchange is found just four verses after the one many use to suggest that Peter was made head of the collective church: "Now I say to you that you are Peter, and upon this rock I will build my church, and all the powers of hell will not conquer it" (v. 18 NLT).

Revelation indicates that when Jesus finally returns to Earth, He won't be a bleeding-heart antiwar activist. He will make war and smite the nations with a sharp sword, rule people with a rod of iron, and tread the winepress of the fierceness and wrath of the almighty God.

> And I saw heaven opened, and behold a white horse; and he that sat upon him was called Faithful and True, and in righteousness he doth judge and make war. His eyes were as a flame of fire, and on his head were many crowns; and he had a name written, that no man knew, but he himself. And he was clothed with a vesture dipped in blood: and his name is called The Word of God. And the armies which were in heaven followed him upon white horses, clothed in fine linen, white and clean. And out of his mouth goeth a sharp sword, that with it he should smite the nations: and he shall rule them with a rod of iron: and he treadeth the winepress of the fierceness and wrath of Almighty God. And he hath on his vesture and on his thigh a name written, KING OF KINGS, AND LORD OF LORDS. (19:11–16)

And Isaiah says that Jesus will "slay the wicked" upon His return: "He shall smite the earth with the rod of his mouth, and with the breath of his lips shall he slay the wicked" (11:4).

Verse after verse provides a clear indication of a key aspect of the personality of God: He can get angry to the point of killing people. It's a part of God's nature that leaves some confused or even upset.

Many churchgoers have learned for years that God is all about love, mercy, and forgiveness; that He is kind and gentle-hearted all the time; that He accepts everyone as they are; and that He is tolerant of all things, despite the absence of the word *tolerant* in Scripture. Some never hear all the facts, or they choose to ignore them. God could have forgiven the people of Noah's day, or the people of Sodom and Gomorrah. But He did not. He put them to death. Perhaps the God many think they have known for so long is very different from the God of the Bible.

One thing is certain: if we refuse to change our lives and live according to God's instructions, we shall also be killed by the Creator. Jesus said so Himself, twice. "Except ye repent, ye shall all likewise perish" (Luke 13:3, 5).

But God practically begs people to be obedient, so they will *not* suffer the penalty of death.

I call heaven and earth to record this day against you, that I have set before you life and death, blessing and cursing: therefore choose life, that both thou and thy seed may live. (Deuteronomy 30:19)

For I take no pleasure in the death of anyone, declares the Sovereign LORD. Repent and live! (Ezekiel 18:32 NIV)

Even Moses Was on God's Hit List

Is it possible that God actually wanted to kill His friend Moses? After all, Moses, the man chosen to lead the people of God out of slavery in Egypt, is considered one of the greatest heroes of the entire Bible.

The brief account is found in Exodus, shortly after God spoke to Moses from a burning bush. On his way back to Egypt with orders to lead the Israelites to freedom, Moses was traveling with his wife, Zipporah, and their son. Thrust into the story of Moses' divine mission is this stunning verse: "On the journey, when Moses and his family had stopped for the night, the LORD confronted Moses and was about to kill him" (4:24 NLT).

As surprising at it sounds, it nevertheless is there in all translations of the Bible. The King James Version states that "the LORD met him, and sought to kill him."

How could Moses, just dispatched by God for the crucial assignment of leading the people of Israel to freedom, end up on God's most wanted list? Was it a mistake? A misunderstanding? A typographical error of the worst kind? None of those. God was indeed about to kill Moses. The next two verses explain why.

> But Zipporah, his wife, took a flint knife and circumcised her son. She threw the foreskin at Moses' feet and said, "What a blood-smeared bridegroom you are to me!" [When she called Moses a "blood-smeared bridegroom," she was referring to the circumcision.] After that, the LORD left him alone. (vv. 25–26 NLT)

God was about to execute Moses because Moses had not circumcised his son. Apparently, Moses' wife knew precisely why God was angry with her husband; she jumped to the rescue, immediately grabbing a flint knife to complete the task herself. The commandment to circumcise was part of the original covenant God made with Abraham in Genesis.

> This is my covenant, which ye shall keep, between me and you and thy seed after thee; every man child among you shall be circumcised. And ye shall circumcise the flesh of your foreskin; and it shall be a token of the covenant betwixt me and you. (17:10–11)

Moses was a direct descendant of Abraham, being born of the tribe of Levi, one of Abraham's twelve great-grandsons.

Zipporah was livid that Moses had not obeyed God sooner, so she took matters into her own hands, literally, and sliced off her son's foreskin. She then flung it at Moses' feet and began ripping him a new one, so to speak, twice calling him a "bloody husband" (KJV). The point of the whole episode, though, is that God could not expect the Israelites to follow Moses' instructions if Moses, their appointed leader, willfully disobeyed God. As soon as the circumcision was completed by the angry Zipporah, the case was closed, and God no longer sought to kill Moses.

God Sought to Slay All His People—Twice!

Moses was not the only one on God's hit list. In fact, God wanted to kill the entire nation of Israel. And His anger rose this high not once but at least twice, showing how angry God can really become even with the people He loves and is trying to lead to salvation. The incidents are recorded in the first few books of the Bible, with the initial blowup mentioned in Exodus and a near repeat performance highlighted in Numbers.

In Exodus, the problem began when Moses stayed on Mount Sinai for forty days, communing with God and receiving the Ten Commandments. While he was away, many of his fellow Israelites grew impatient, not knowing what had happened to him, and they convinced Moses' brother, Aaron, to fashion an idol in the form of a calf. To make matters worse, the Israelites associated their true God with the idol by declaring their celebration of this idol as a festival to honor the real God.

When Aaron saw how excited the people were about it, he built an altar in front of the calf and announced, "Tomorrow there will be a festival to the Lord!" (32:5 NLT).

God was not happy with this festival—even though it was dedicated to Him—since a golden calf was given the credit and honor for leading the people out of slavery in Egypt.

> And the Lord said unto Moses, Go, get thee down; for thy people, which thou broughtest out of the land of Egypt, have corrupted themselves: they have turned aside quickly out of the way which I commanded them: they have made them a molten calf, and have worshipped it, and have sacrificed thereunto, and said, These be thy gods, O Israel, which have brought thee up out of the land of Egypt. (vv. 7–8)

Enough was enough, God felt, and He looked to kill, slaughter, waste, eliminate—however you wish to say it—His entire populace, with the exception of one man. "And the Lord said unto Moses, I have seen this people, and, behold, it is a stiffnecked people: now therefore let me alone, that my wrath may wax hot against them, and that I may consume them: and I will make of thee a great nation" (vv. 9–10).

The New Living Translation makes the meaning unmistakable: "Then the Lord said, "I have seen how stubborn and rebellious these people are. Now leave me alone so my anger can blaze against them and destroy them all. Then I will make you, Moses, into a great nation instead of them" (vv. 9–10).

The God who had led hundreds of thousands of His people out of captivity, who had inflicted terrible plagues on the Egyptians before drowning their army in the Red Sea, now wanted to slay all the descendants of Jacob in one fell swoop, to begin again with a clean slate and rebuild His nation with Moses as the starting point!

What some may find equally astounding is that Moses succeeded in changing God's mind about the mass execution.

> And Moses besought the LORD his God, and said, LORD, why doth thy wrath wax hot against thy people, which thou hast brought forth out of the land of Egypt with great power, and with a mighty hand? Wherefore should the Egyptians speak, and say, For mischief did he bring them out, to slay them in the mountains, and to consume them from the face of the earth? Turn from thy fierce wrath, and repent of this evil against thy people. Remember Abraham, Isaac, and Israel, thy servants, to whom thou swarest by thine own self, and saidst unto them, I will multiply your seed as the stars of heaven, and all this land that I have spoken of will I give unto your seed, and they shall inherit it for ever. And the LORD repented of the evil which he thought to do unto his people. (vv. 11–14)

Apparently, we human beings can change God's mind when we reason with Him logically. Moses suggested to God that it would not look good among the pagan peoples of the Earth to know that God brought His people out of slavery, only to destroy them in the wilderness. Moses also reminded God of the covenant made with the patriarchs—he wanted those promises to be fulfilled.

Of course, Moses himself was a descendant of Abraham, Isaac, and Jacob. He was a member of the tribe of Levi, one of Jacob's twelve sons. So even if God were to slay everyone else, He still could have fulfilled the promises to the patriarchs through Moses. It just would have taken a little longer.

But Moses went far beyond two rhetorical arguments to stave off the execution. He actually offered to trade his own eternal salvation in the future kingdom of God for the lives of his fellow Israelites. "And Moses returned unto the LORD, and said, Oh, this people have sinned a great sin, and have made them gods of gold. Yet now, if thou wilt forgive their sin—; and if not, blot me, I pray thee, out of thy book which thou hast written" (vv. 31–32).

The book Moses is talking about is the Book of Life, a listing of those who are granted eternal life by the gift of God. It's mentioned six times in Revelation, with citations such as "And whosoever was not found written in the book of life was cast into the lake of fire" (20:15).

What Moses said apparently worked, because the people were given a stay of execution, at least temporarily.

And the LORD said unto Moses, Whosoever hath sinned against me, him will I blot out of my book. Therefore now go, lead the people unto the place of which I have spoken unto thee: behold, mine Angel shall go before thee: nevertheless in the day when I visit I will visit their sin upon them. And the LORD plagued the people, because they made the calf, which Aaron made. (Exodus 32:33–35)

Though God spared the vast majority of Israelites, it's important to note that not everyone got off scot-free. The golden calf was burned up and ground into powder that was added to the water of the Israelites, who were then forced to drink it. God also ordered the execution of some three thousand.

And he said unto them, Thus saith the LORD God of Israel, Put every man his sword by his side, and go in and out from gate to gate throughout the camp, and slay every man his brother, and every man his companion, and every man his neighbour. And the children of Levi did according to the word of Moses: and there fell of the people that day about three thousand men. (vv. 27–28)

This incident with the golden calf was not the only time God sought to execute His entire nation. Strangely enough, after all that unpleasantness, it happened again.

The second instance came on the heels of a rebellion against Moses. An Israelite named Korah convinced some 250 men to join him in a challenge to God's appointed leaders. Korah reasoned that God had set *all* of the people apart for sanctification, not just Moses and Aaron. Korah felt that those two were putting themselves above everyone else.

The sentiment of the disgruntled was summed up by one of Korah's fellow rebels, Dathan, who said, "Is it a small thing that thou hast brought us up out of a land that floweth with milk and honey, to kill us in the wilderness, except thou make thyself altogether a prince over us?" (Numbers 16:13).

Moses warned others to stay away from the tents of Korah and the rebels, because he knew God would punish them for their uprising. God sent fire from heaven to consume them, and split the ground open to swallow not only the whole gang of evil challengers but everything they owned.

> And the earth opened her mouth, and swallowed them up, and their houses, and all the men that appertained unto Korah, and all their goods. They, and all that appertained to them, went down alive into the pit, and the earth closed upon them: and they perished from among the congregation. And all Israel that were round about them fled at the cry of them: for they said, Lest the earth swallow us up also. And there came out a fire from the LORD, and consumed the two hundred and fifty men that offered incense. (vv. 32–35)

In an instant, 250 Israelites were buried alive by God for challenging Moses' authority. Despite this earth-shaking catastrophe, the people still did not learn their lesson, and the next day they blamed Moses and Aaron for the disaster. God again appeared on the scene and sought to destroy all the Israelites with the exception of Moses.

> But on the morrow all the congregation of the children of Israel murmured against Moses and against Aaron, saying, Ye have killed the people of the LORD. And it came to pass, when the congregation was gathered against Moses and against Aaron, that they looked toward the tabernacle of the congregation: and, behold, the cloud covered it, and the glory of the LORD appeared . . . And the LORD spake unto Moses, saying, Get you up from among this congregation, that I may consume them as in a moment. (vv. 41–45)

As He had in the golden calf scenario, God was ready to exterminate His whole nation and warned Moses to get away from the rest of the people in order to spare his life.

The people of Israel were not as fortunate this time. Moses instructed Aaron to grab an incense burner loaded with coals from the altar and carry it among the people to try to save them from impending destruction, saying

Go quickly unto the congregation, and make an atonement for them: for there is wrath gone out from the LORD; the plague is begun. And Aaron took as Moses commanded, and ran into the midst of the congregation; and, behold, the plague was begun among the people: and he put on incense, and made an atonement for the people. And he stood between the dead and the living; and the plague was stayed. Now they that died in the plague were fourteen thousand and seven hundred, beside them that died about the matter of Korah. And Aaron returned unto Moses unto the door of the tabernacle of the congregation: and the plague was stayed. (vv. 46–50)

Moses did not use rhetoric to reason with God, as he had when the Lord first sought to obliterate the nation. God gave a virtually instant death penalty to some 14,700 rebellious Israelites, in addition to the 250 slain the day before in Korah's offensive, bringing the total death toll in two consecutive days to just fewer than 15,000. Had it not been for Moses and Aaron's actions in atoning for the people, God may have consumed the entire nation.

The God of the Bible is not only the Creator of life, He is the one who can and does take it away. He is the one who has killed more men than Cecil B. DeMille ever did on film. I am in no way suggesting God did not have good reason to do what He did. After all, He is God. But if people are going to believe the Bible, they must stop believing the fairy tale that none of this nastiness took place—and could again.

Remember, it was Jesus Christ who said unless we all repent and follow God, we will all likewise perish.

CHAPTER SIXTEEN

DA JESUS CODE

IN THE PAST FEW YEARS, there has been incredible controversy over *The Da Vinci Code*. The book and movie of that name suggested a trail of coded information proving that Jesus married and had children. Of course, none of that is biblical.

But while *The Da Vinci Code* is fiction, many do not realize Jesus Himself spoke in secret, coded messages during His life on Earth. Call it "Da Jesus Code."

Got Jesus?

As strange as it sounds, no one understood Jesus in His day. Not the people He addressed, not even His own apostles. They simply did not understand Him. And Jesus meant it to be this way. He intentionally prevented most people from understanding His message!

To make sense of this point, we need to know that Jesus spoke in parables—earthly stories containing a spiritual truth about the kingdom of God. Parables are essentially analogies. Though the exact figure varies depending on one's definition of a parable, there are some fifty parables found in the pages of Scripture. Over the years, some of them, such as the prodigal son, mustard seed, and good Samaritan stories, have become so well-known that they have transcended the Bible and now appear in everyday discourse.

Many Christians today assume Jesus spoke in parables to allow confused people to "get it," to help them understand what He was saying. They believe the Son of God talked in simple terms, using everyday expressions even common folks would understand. It sounds like a very "Christian" thing to do.

Secret Agent Man

However, when asked why He spoke in parables, Jesus gave the exact opposite reason, saying He did *not* want most people to "get it." He was speaking in code to actually prevent them from understanding: "And the disciples came, and said unto him, Why speakest thou unto them in parables? He answered and said unto them, Because it is given unto you to know the mysteries of the kingdom of heaven, but to them it is not given" (Matthew 13:10–11).

Jesus explained that He was unlocking the mysteries of the kingdom to His few chosen disciples, but was concealing them from everyone else. As He said, "To them it is not given."

Jesus continued:

> For whosoever hath, to him shall be given, and he shall have more abundance: but whosoever hath not, from him shall be taken away even that he hath. Therefore speak I to them in parables: because they seeing see not; and hearing they hear not, neither do they understand. And in them is fulfilled the prophecy of Esaias, which saith, By hearing ye shall hear, and shall not understand; and seeing ye shall see, and shall not perceive: For this people's heart is waxed gross, and their ears are dull of hearing, and their eyes they have closed; lest at any time they should see with their eyes and hear with their ears, and should understand with their heart, and should be converted, and I should heal them. (vv. 12–15)

Mark recorded Jesus' statement in similar fashion:

> And he said unto them, Unto you it is given to know the mystery of the kingdom of God: but unto them that are without, all these things are done in parables: that seeing they may see, and not perceive; and hearing they may hear, and not understand; lest at any time they should be converted, and their sins should be forgiven them. (4:11–12)

Jesus explained that Isaiah had prophesied that people would hear the teaching of God but not understand it. Moreover, He explained that He spoke in parables lest (for fear that) people should see, convert, and become healed and forgiven. He did not want them to be forgiven at that time! The New Living Translation makes it absolutely clear that Jesus was intentionally hiding information. Here are those same two verses:

He replied, "You are permitted to understand the secret about the Kingdom of God. But I am using these stories to conceal everything about it from outsiders, so that the Scriptures might be fulfilled: 'They see what I do, but they don't perceive its meaning. They hear my words, but they don't understand. So they will not turn from their sins and be forgiven.'"

Of course, since nothing is too hard for God, He could have been the greatest communicator in history. He could have clearly explained everything He said. Instead, He chose to speak in coded fashion to confound the mysteries of the kingdom for those not called at that time. He prevented the information from being crystal clear, the direct opposite of what many people today claim is the reason He spoke in parables. Now, just how many people had an inkling about Jesus' mission during His ministry? As you're about to see, the number is a few more than most may assume.

CHAPTER SEVENTEEN

JESUS' OTHER APOSTLES

QUICK! How many eggs are in a dozen? How many months are there in a year? How many people did Jesus specifically appoint and dispatch to preach the good news about the kingdom of God during His earthly ministry? And how many licks does it take to get to the Tootsie Roll center of a Tootsie Pop?

The world may never know the answer to that last question, but the others do have answers.

While any fourth grader knows there are twelve eggs in a dozen and twelve months in a year, it's quite easy for Bible readers to assume Jesus sent out twelve people to preach His message. After all, most everyone has heard of the twelve apostles, or disciples. Indeed, there were twelve men specifically named as apostles, but this number does not include a large group of other "mystery men" Jesus sent on a special mission.

The word *apostle* means delegate or messenger, a person sent forth with orders. There are four verses in the King James Bible that display the words *twelve* and *apostles* in the same sentence, including the sixth chapter of Luke's gospel:

> And when it was day, he called unto him his disciples: and of them he chose twelve, whom also he named apostles; Simon, (whom he also named Peter,) and Andrew his brother, James and John, Philip and

Bartholomew, Matthew and Thomas, James the son of Alphaeus, and Simon called Zelotes, and Judas the brother of James, and Judas Iscariot, which also was the traitor. (vv. 13–16)

In the ninth chapter of Luke, Jesus dispatched this dozen with explicit instructions:

Then he called his twelve disciples together, and gave them power and authority over all devils, and to cure diseases. And he sent them to preach the kingdom of God, and to heal the sick. And he said unto them, Take nothing for your journey, neither staves, nor scrip, neither bread, neither money; neither have two coats apiece. And whatsoever house ye enter into, there abide, and thence depart. And whosoever will not receive you, when ye go out of that city, shake off the very dust from your feet for a testimony against them. And they departed, and went through the towns, preaching the gospel, and healing every where. (vv. 1–6)

The Second String

Apparently, it was just the beginning of Jesus' sending people out; in the very next chapter of Luke, we are told of a special group of seventy other people (some manuscripts put the number at seventy-two) whom Jesus chose for precisely the same mission as the first group of twelve.

After these things the LORD appointed other seventy also, and sent them two and two before his face into every city and place, whither he himself would come. (10:1)

After this the Lord appointed seventy-two others and sent them two by two ahead of him to every town and place where he was about to go. (NIV)

The directions He gave to this large gang sound very similar to the instructions handed to the twelve apostles a chapter earlier.

Therefore said he unto them, The harvest truly is great, but the labourers are few: pray ye therefore the Lord of the harvest, that he would send forth labourers into his harvest. Go your ways: behold, I send you forth as lambs among wolves. Carry neither purse, nor scrip, nor shoes: and salute no man by the way. And into whatsoever house ye enter, first say, Peace be to this house. And if the son of peace be there, your peace shall rest upon it: if not, it shall turn to you again. And in the same house remain, eating and drinking such things as they give: for the labourer is worthy of his hire. Go not from house to house. And into whatsoever city ye enter, and they receive you, eat such things as are set before you: And heal the sick that are therein, and say unto them, The kingdom of God is come nigh unto you. But into whatsoever city ye enter, and they receive you not, go your ways out into the streets of the same, and say, Even the very dust of your city, which cleaveth on us, we do wipe off against you: notwithstanding be ye sure of this, that the kingdom of God is come nigh unto you. (vv. 2–11)

The number in the group is repeated later in the chapter when they came back to report good news to Jesus.

And the seventy returned again with joy, saying, Lord, even the devils are subject unto us through thy name. (v. 17)

The seventy-two returned with joy and said, "Lord, even the demons submit to us in your name." (NIV)

The gospel never names these other apostles, but it's possible two of them are identified later in the Bible. After the death and resurrection of Jesus, the apostles sought to replace one of their original twelve, since Judas had committed suicide. They asked God to help them with their decision, as recorded in Acts.

Two men were considered for their replacement, as they had been with the original group from the baptism of John:

Wherefore of these men which have companied with us all the time that the Lord Jesus went in and out among us, beginning from the baptism of John, unto that same day that he was taken up from us, must one be ordained to be a witness with us of his resurrection. And they appointed two, Joseph called Barsabas, who was surnamed Justus, and Matthias.

And they prayed, and said, Thou, Lord, which knowest the hearts of all men, shew whether of these two thou hast chosen, that he may take part of this ministry and apostleship, from which Judas by transgression fell, that he might go to his own place. And they gave forth their lots; and the lot fell upon Matthias; and he was numbered with the eleven apostles. (1:21–26)

While I have used the term *mystery men* to describe these evangelists, there is no way to know if the group was exclusively made up of male preachers. The Scripture gives no indication if they were men, women, or a combination of both.

But the point is that up to six dozen other disciples —that is to say, students or followers of Jesus—were specifically assigned by Him to preach the gospel of the kingdom while Jesus was still on Earth. The famous twelve apostles were only the beginning.

CHAPTER EIGHTEEN

IMAGE IS EVERYTHING

DID YOU KNOW that God never said, "Let Me make man in My image" while He was creating the world?

I know it sounds like a very famous quote from Scripture, and you may have assumed for years that it was in there. Feel free to run to your Bible right now if you wish to check, but trust me, it's not there. It's not in the book of Genesis, and not in the gospel of John. The phrase is *nowhere* in the Bible.

The exact statement God used as He created the human race is this: "Let us make man in our image, after our likeness" (Genesis 1:26).

If your eyes glossed over that and you did not catch the difference, I will spell it out for you. God did NOT say, "Let ME make man in MY image, after MY likeness." He said, "Let US make man in OUR image, after OUR likeness."

The words are only slightly different, but they make a significant difference regarding who or what God is, and the reason men and women were created by God in the first place. This one phrase in the Bible is the starting point for the truth about why we're all here. Though it has only a few words, those words contain volumes of information.

It's All About "Us"

Let's start with the words *us* and *our*. They're obviously plural. In fact, the word translated as "God" in the verse is *Elohim*, which is also plural in the Hebrew language. It indicates more than one. Thus, there is more than one member in the God Family.

Additionally, the phrase "Let us make man in our image, after our likeness" makes it clear that human beings actually look like God, and God looks like us. Think of it this way: if someone paints your portrait, you just might hear, "That's a very good likeness of you." That's assuming, of course, that the artist has some talent and does not paint you like a circus clown. When someone says it's a good likeness, it means it looks like you.

There's a New Kind in Town

God was explaining that human beings were made in His image and likeness. We were not made to look like dogs, cats, trees, or tarantulas. Those other living things were also created by God, but they were not made to look like Him. Genesis 1:26 follows a series of pronouncements with which God had created a planet full of items such as plants and animals, all after *their own kind.*

And God said, Let the earth bring forth grass, the herb yielding seed, and the fruit tree yielding fruit after his kind, whose seed is in itself, upon the earth: and it was so. (v. 11)

And God created great whales, and every living creature that moveth, which the waters brought forth abundantly, after their kind, and every winged fowl after his kind: and God saw that it was good. (v. 21)

And God made the beast of the earth after his kind, and cattle after their kind, and every thing that creepeth upon the earth after his kind: and God saw that it was good. (v. 25)

However, when it came to making human beings, men and women were created in *God's* image. Here's more of the text:

And God said, Let us make man in our image, after our likeness: and let them have dominion over the fish of the sea, and over the fowl of the air, and over the cattle, and over all the earth, and over every creeping thing that creepeth upon the earth. So God created man in his own image, in the image of God created he him; male and female created he them. (vv. 26–27)

It's unmistakable. Scripture says God created animals after the animal kind. He created trees after the tree kind. But He created humans in His own image, after the God kind.

He's Got the Body of a God

The Bible is sprinkled with references to God's body features. And guess what? They happen to look like the parts of the human body. That's not to suggest those parts are made of flesh and blood, but they nevertheless appear like our own parts. For instance, God has:

A HEAD, with HAIR (God is not bald.)

Ephraim also is the strength of mine head. (Psalm 60:7)

For he put on righteousness as a breastplate, and a helmet of salvation upon his head. (Isaiah 59:17)

His head and his hairs were white like wool. (Revelation 1:14)

A FACE

For we will destroy this place, because the cry of them is waxen great before the face of the LORD. (Genesis 19:13)

And the LORD spake unto Moses face to face, as a man speaketh unto his friend. (Exodus 33:11)

The LORD make his face shine upon thee, and be gracious unto thee. (Numbers 6:25)

. . . a people that provoketh me to anger continually to my face. (Isaiah 65:3)

EYES

But Noah found grace in the eyes of the LORD. (Genesis 6:8)

The eyes of the LORD are in every place, beholding the evil and the good. (Proverbs 15:3)

His eyes were as a flame of fire. (Revelation 1:14)

A MOUTH

And the glory of the LORD shall be revealed, and all flesh shall see it together: for the mouth of the LORD hath spoken it. (Isaiah 40:5)

But he answered and said, It is written, Man shall not live by bread alone, but by every word that proceedeth out of the mouth of God. (Matthew 4:4)

LIPS

But oh that God would speak, and open his lips against thee. (Job 11:5)

By the word of thy lips I have kept me from the paths of the destroyer. (Psalm 17:4)

A VOICE

And they heard the voice of the LORD God walking in the garden in the cool of the day. (Genesis 3:8)

And all these blessings shall come on thee, and overtake thee, if thou shalt hearken unto the voice of the LORD thy God. (Deuteronomy 28:2)

Moses spake, and God answered him by a voice. (Exodus 19:19)

. . . his voice as the sound of many waters. (Revelation 1:15)

A NOSE, with NOSTRILS

These are a smoke in my nose, a fire that burneth all the day. (Isaiah 65:5)

And with the blast of thy nostrils the waters were gathered together. (Exodus 15:8)

HANDS

But when he seeth his children, the work of mine hands, in the midst of him, they shall sanctify my name, and sanctify the Holy One of Jacob, and shall fear the God of Israel. (Isaiah 29:23)

It is a fearful thing to fall into the hands of the living God. (Hebrews 10:31)

FINGERS

When I consider thy heavens, the work of thy fingers, the moon and the stars, which thou hast ordained. (Psalm 8:3)

And he gave unto Moses, when he had made an end of communing with him upon mount Sinai, two tables of testimony, tables of stone, written with the finger of God. (Exodus 31:18)

FEET

The LORD hath his way in the whirlwind and in the storm, and the clouds are the dust of his feet. (Nahum 1:3)

And his feet shall stand in that day upon the mount of Olives. (Zechariah 14:4)

And his feet like unto fine brass, as if they burned in a furnace. (Revelation 1:15)

To drive the point home, in the heart of the Old Testament, the prophet Ezekiel saw "the appearance of the likeness of the glory of the LORD" and noted that "upon the likeness of the throne was the likeness as the appearance of a man above upon it" (Ezekiel 1:26–28).

Yes, ladies and gents, God looks like a human being, and human beings look like God! But is there any significance to it?

The Family of God

As shocking as this may sound, the reason we look like God and were made in His image is because we were created to be part of the actual Family of God and live with Him in eternity. We were not fashioned like the rest of the animals to live and die with no higher purpose. We were designed with the same features as God, because we will actually be born into His family—the same family as Jesus Christ!

In Hebrews, we read:

> Both the one who makes men holy and those who are made holy are of the same family. So Jesus is not ashamed to call them brothers. He says, "I will declare your name to my brothers; in the presence of the congregation I will sing your praises." And again, "I will put my trust in him." And again he says, "Here am I, and the children God has given me." (2:11–13 NIV)

Of course, this does not mean that we will become God the Father or Jesus. But it does mean what it says, that we are the brothers of Jesus Christ, actual children of God in the Family of God:

> And I will be your Father, and you will be my sons and daughters, says the Lord Almighty. (2 Corinthians 6:18 NLT)

> Blessed are the peacemakers: for they shall be called the children of God. (Matthew 5:9)

> But as many as received him, to them gave he power to become the sons of God. (John 1:12)

> For ye are all the children of God by faith in Christ Jesus. (Galatians 3:26)

And just as earthly children get all the rights and privileges that come from being their parents' sons and daughters, God's children receive benefits from being related to Him:

> Neither can they die any more . . . and are the children of God, being the children of the resurrection. (Luke 20:36)

> The Spirit itself beareth witness with our spirit, that we are the children of God: and if children, then heirs; heirs of God, and joint-heirs with Christ; if so be that we suffer with him, that we may be also glorified together. (Romans 8:16–17)

It's amazing to me how people can easily accept a saying such as "we are all God's children," yet not truly grasp its significance.

The phrase means, of course, that we literally are God's children, His sons and daughters, descendants, or however else you can say offspring of parents. The New Testament even uses that specific word: "for we are also his offspring" (Acts 17:28).

Just as human children resemble their human parents, just as they are part of the same family, so humans who follow God are part of God's family.

There will be millions and perhaps billions of humans born into the Family of God. And there will still be only one God, because remember, God is a family. It is a plural word meaning more than one in that family.

It makes sense why God has names like Father and Son and uses terms like *brothers* and *children*. These are *family* terms.

The human destiny is not to wither away and die and become food for the worms forever. It's not even to float on clouds and play harps 24/7. Humans have the potential to be children of God, eternally living members of His family, doing what God does!

I know it sounds shocking. But the Bible does not use phrases such as "children of God" or "sons of God" because it wants to sound cute, warm and fuzzy, or majestic. It is telling us our destiny. And just because we currently have mortal, flesh-and-blood bodies that sometimes creak with arthritic pain, it does not mean it will always be that way. We shall all be changed.

The apostle John explains it this way: "Beloved, now are we the sons of God, and it doth not yet appear what we shall be: but we know that, when he shall appear, we shall be like him; for we shall see him as he is" (1 John 3:2).

People who follow God in this life already belong to the Family of God, but they don't see right now what they will eventually become because they're still in their current, mortal, *flesh-and-blood* bodies. But that will change once Jesus returns. Dead people will be resurrected and given new, eternally alive bodies composed not of flesh and blood but of spirit. We will finally see God as He really is, because we will be on the same immortal plane.

Jesus Himself spoke about this, noting that people would have to be born of spirit in order to be in God's kingdom: "Except a man be born of water and of the Spirit, he cannot enter into the kingdom of God. That which is born of the flesh is flesh; and that which is born of the Spirit is spirit" (John 3:5–6).

Every human being on Earth is currently mortal and consists of flesh and blood. We were born that way from our flesh-and-blood parents. But God, who is an eternal Spirit, is offering us eternal life in a new, immortal body that consists of spirit.

A Body to Die For

The apostle Paul explained that God will change the bodies of believers from mortal ones, made of skin, muscles, bones, and blood, into immortal ones, made up of spirit, just as God is immortal and consists of spirit. Why is that so essential? Because, as Paul stated outright, "flesh and blood cannot inherit the kingdom of God" (1 Corinthians 15:50).

The Bible means what it says. People who make it to the kingdom of God will no longer be made of flesh and blood, but spirit! Yet they will still have the ability to appear in physical bodies, just as Jesus and the angels have been shown to do in both the Old and New Testaments. Here's Paul's opinion on our future bodies once the kingdom arrives:

> There are bodies in the heavens, and there are bodies on earth. The glory of the heavenly bodies is different from the beauty of the earthly bodies . . . It is the same way for the resurrection of the dead. Our earthly bodies, which die and decay, will be different when they are resurrected, for they will never die. Our bodies now disappoint us, but when they are raised, they will be full of glory. They are weak now, but when they are raised, they will be full of power. They are natural human bodies now, but when they are raised, they will be spiritual bodies. For just as there

are natural bodies, so also there are spiritual bodies. (1 Corinthians 15:40–44 NLT)

Just as we are now like Adam, the man of the earth, so we will someday be like Christ, the man from heaven. What I am saying, dear brothers and sisters, is that flesh and blood cannot inherit the Kingdom of God. These perishable bodies of ours are not able to live forever. But let me tell you a wonderful secret God has revealed to us. Not all of us will die, but we will all be transformed. It will happen in a moment, in the blinking of an eye, when the last trumpet is blown. For when the trumpet sounds, the Christians who have died will be raised with transformed bodies. And then we who are living will be transformed so that we will never die. For our perishable earthly bodies must be transformed into heavenly bodies that will never die. (vv. 49–53 NLT)

When believers are given eternal life, their bodies will appear in the same general form that they had all their lives. For instance, each will still have a head, face, torso, two arms, two legs, etc. But now believers will be born of the spirit and exist in a glorified form. Remember, we look like God and He looks like us, because we were created in His image and likeness!

Jesus Christ died and has already been resurrected into His glorified, immortal body. Paul called Him "the firstborn," with many more human beings to follow and become His brothers and sisters: "For God knew his people in advance, and he chose them to become like his Son, so that his Son would be the firstborn, with many brothers and sisters" (Romans 8:29 NLT).

Consider also what the author of Hebrews wrote:

For somewhere in the Scriptures it says, "What is man that you should think of him, and the son of man that you should care for him? For a little while you made him lower than the angels, and you crowned him with glory and honor. You gave him authority over all things." Now when it says "all things," it means nothing is left out. But we have not yet seen all of this happen. (2:6–8 NLT)

Read that over again slowly so you can really absorb the incredible truth. The answer to the question, *what is man?* is that he is a being that is "lower than the angels"—for a little while. The "little while" spoken of in this verse is the human life span. But once we die, we will eventually be *above* the angels—members of God's family and known as the children of God. We have been given authority over all created things. That means everything. Nothing has been left out. But we will not see all of this take place until Jesus returns and we become born into our brand-new, eternal bodies made of spirit to live forever with Jesus Christ, our fellow member of God's family.

Many of you have never heard this message. But it's right there on the pages of your own Bible. Whether or not you choose to believe it is up to you.

Jobs of the Future

If you ever wondered what you might be doing for all eternity, it's not an extended vacation of looking at Jesus slide shows and singing songs, such as "Michael Row the Boat Ashore." And it won't be polishing pearly gates. There is important work that needs to be done. For instance, did you know that resurrected humans will have duties that include judging the world's citizens and the activities of angels? Read Paul's stunning statement for yourself: "Don't you know that someday we Christians are going to judge the world? . . . Don't you realize that we Christians will judge angels?" (1 Corinthians 6:2–3 NLT).

Jesus Himself also said His followers would be given *rulership* in the kingdom of God:

And he that overcometh, and keepeth my works unto the end, to him will I give power over the nations: and he shall rule them with a rod of iron; as the vessels of a potter shall they be broken to shivers: even as I received of my Father . . . To him that overcometh will I grant to sit with me in my throne, even as I also overcame, and am set down with my Father in his throne. (Revelation 2:26–27; 3:21)

And the apostle John foresaw the resurrected children of God reigning alongside God:

And I saw thrones, and they sat upon them, and judgment was given unto them . . . and they lived and reigned with Christ a thousand years . . . Blessed and holy is he that hath part in the first resurrection: on such the second death hath no power, but they shall be priests of God and of Christ, and shall reign with him a thousand years. (Revelation 20:4, 6)

Finally, Paul said that the whole universe is anxiously waiting for the coming day, when the true and eternal form of the children of God is revealed:

For all creation is waiting eagerly for that future day when God will reveal who his children really are. All creation anticipates the day when it will join God's children in glorious freedom from death and decay. For we know that all creation has been groaning as in the pains of childbirth right up to the present time. And even we Christians, although we have the Holy Spirit within us as a foretaste of future glory, also groan to be released from pain and suffering. We, too, wait anxiously for that day when God will give us our full rights as his children, including the new bodies he has promised us. (Romans 8:19–23 NLT)

It's fantastic. Astonishing. Sensational. Mind-boggling. And it's all in the Bible: "But as it is written, Eye hath not seen, nor ear heard, neither have entered into the heart of man, the things which God hath prepared for them that love him. But God hath revealed them unto us by his Spirit: for the Spirit searcheth all things, yea, the deep things of God" (1 Corinthians 2:9–10).

We were not created in the image or likeness of puppies, no matter how cute and cuddly they can be. We were not created in the image and likeness of butterflies, no matter how beautiful their wings. We were not even created in the image of angels.

God said, "Let us make man in our image, after our likeness." We were created in the image and likeness of the all-knowing, all-loving, eternal God, who is bringing countless members into His family.

Will you be one of them?

CHAPTER NINETEEN

THE BALD AND THE MAULED

HAVE YOU EVER SEEN a bald guy wearing a bad toupee and snickered to yourself? Or have you ever been in public with your children, seen a bald man, and had the kids bark out comments like, "Look at that shiny head!" or, "Get a load of that chrome dome!"? While the kids think it's hilarious to see a man with a cue ball for a noggin, the bald guy is hardly getting a kick out of it.

There's a stunning incident in the Bible involving a bald man who was being teased by a gang of youngsters. What happened to the kids is downright startling, because the man they were making fun of was no ordinary man. He happened to be a prophet of God.

Just two verses of Scripture relay the story. It involved the prophet Elisha, moments after God ended a drought through Elisha's work. Here's how the King James Version renders it:

And he went up from thence unto Bethel: and as he was going up by the way, there came forth little children out of the city, and mocked him, and said unto him, Go up, thou bald head; go up, thou bald head. And he turned back, and looked on them, and cursed them in the name of the LORD. And there came forth two she bears out of the wood, and tare forty and two children of them. (2 Kings 2:23–24)

In more modern English, the New Living Translation:

> Elisha left Jericho and went up to Bethel. As he was walking along the road, a group of boys from the town began mocking and making fun of him. "Go away, you baldhead!" they chanted. "Go away, you baldhead!" Elisha turned around and looked at them, and he cursed them in the name of the Lord. Then two bears came out of the woods and mauled forty-two of them.

God's prophet was apparently in no forgiving mood when these punks made fun of him. He appealed directly to God, who apparently agreed with Elisha, because two bears were immediately dispatched for instant justice, shredding forty-two of them.

The Scripture does not give any further information about this attack; neither does it mention if any died as a result. But it's certainly something to think about the next time you experience an urge to make fun of a bald guy.

CHAPTER TWENTY

STICK IT TO THE MAN

WE HAVE ALL HEARD of strange sentences for criminals, but can you imagine being sentenced to death for the simple act of gathering sticks on a Saturday? Collecting sticks is not like murdering or raping someone. It is just, well, picking up sticks. Is this a case of judges gone wild? Don't jump to a verdict too quickly, because God Himself was the presiding Judge.

The story is found in the book of Numbers, during the time the ancient Israelites were wandering in the desert. It was not so much the act of stick gathering that caused the uproar; it was *when* it was done. A man was doing it on the Sabbath day, God's day of rest.

Here's how Moses recorded the crime and punishment:

> And while the children of Israel were in the wilderness, they found a man that gathered sticks upon the sabbath day. And they that found him gathering sticks brought him unto Moses and Aaron, and unto all the congregation. And they put him in ward, because it was not declared what should be done to him. And the LORD said unto Moses, The man shall be surely put to death: all the congregation shall stone him with stones without the camp. And all the congregation brought him without the camp, and stoned him with stones, and he died; as the LORD commanded Moses. (15:32–36)

Talk about swift justice. There was no circus trial, no endless appeals, no shyster lawyers, no Bronco chase on a highway, no bloody glove, and no TV coverage. The verdict and sentence were handed down by the wisest, most righteous Judge who ever existed—God.

The man who gathered sticks was found to be violating the fourth commandment, which forbade that work be performed on the seventh day of the week.

> Remember to observe the Sabbath day by keeping it holy. Six days a week are set apart for your daily duties and regular work, but the seventh day is a day of rest dedicated to the Lord your God. On that day no one in your household may do any kind of work. This includes you, your sons and daughters, your male and female servants, your livestock, and any foreigners living among you. For in six days the Lord made the heavens, the earth, the sea, and everything in them; then he rested on the seventh day. That is why the Lord blessed the Sabbath day and set it apart as holy. (Exodus 20:8–11 NLT)

Keep in mind that the Israelites in the desert were not living in cities and commuting to the convenience store. They were together in a large camp in the wilderness, being cared for by God. They did not have to worry about food, since God miraculously provided manna and quail from heaven. All they had to do was obey God's instructions, and all would be well. Yet this Israelite man, for some unspecified reason, decided he would collect wood on the seventh day of the week.

God did not say the man should be shunned, banished, tortured, or jailed. He did not suggest a fine to include court costs. He did not order community service, and He certainly did not forgive him. God sentenced him to death by stoning, and everyone became executioners for a day.

God commanded "all the congregation" to take part in the ultimate punishment, "and all the congregation brought him without the camp, and stoned him with stones, and he died."

The next time capital punishment is in the news, or there's a story about someone in a distant land being stoned to death, keep this event in mind. The loving God of all eternity, Jesus Christ, had no problem killing a man simply for picking up sticks on the day of rest, and He had everyone take part in the execution. It's all in the Bible.

CHAPTER TWENTY-ONE

GOD RAN THE LOTTERY

I AM REALLY MIFFED. I did not win the jackpot in this week's lottery drawing. But most other people who had tickets didn't win the big one either, so that makes me feel a little better.

I think it's strange how some people have no problem with lotteries or gambling, and others suggest they are a sin. So what does the Bible say about it?

To start, while there is no mention of a casino in Scripture, there is extensive discussion about one form of gambling: casting lots. Our modern word *lottery* comes from casting lots, an ancient method of randomly determining the answer to a question.

Though it often surprises people, there is no biblical condemnation of lots or lotteries. In fact, God is presented as a "lottery director" of sorts, instructing His people to hold lotteries—with Himself playing the role of "Determinator"—as their outcomes demonstrate His will. In both the Old and New Testaments, God's people are seen casting lots to determine the will of God.

The first mention has to do with the selection of the so-called scapegoat on one of God's annual holy days, the Day of Atonement.

The original high priest of the ancient Israelites, Moses' brother, Aaron, was instructed to take "two goats, and present them before the LORD at the door of the tabernacle of the congregation." God continued:

And Aaron shall cast lots upon the two goats; one lot for the LORD, and the other lot for the scapegoat. And Aaron shall bring the goat upon which the LORD's lot fell, and offer him for a sin offering. But the goat, on which the lot fell to be the scapegoat, shall be presented alive before the LORD, to make an atonement with him, and to let him go for a scapegoat into the wilderness. (Leviticus 16:7–10)

Later, as the Israelites were taking possession of the promised land, God instructed them to finish dividing their inherited property by casting lots: "Joshua charged them that went to describe the land, saying, Go and walk through the land, and describe it, and come again to me, that I may here cast lots for you before the LORD in Shiloh" (Joshua 18:8).

Once the men had scoped out the region and recorded the property's description, "Joshua cast lots for them in Shiloh before the LORD: and there Joshua divided the land unto the children of Israel according to their divisions" (v. 10).

Israel's first king, Saul, asked God to direct the outcome of a lottery in his quest to determine who had sinned, and the lot correctly pinpointed his own son, Jonathan: "Therefore Saul said unto the LORD God of Israel, Give a perfect lot. And Saul and Jonathan were taken: but the people escaped. And Saul said, Cast lots between me and Jonathan my son. And Jonathan was taken" (1 Samuel 14:41–42).

Jonah Hit the Lottery

Even in the famous story of Jonah, the reluctant prophet who ran away from his appointed mission, a lottery was employed. A life-threatening storm endangered Jonah's getaway ship, and those on board cast lots to find out who was responsible for the tempest. Jonah was correctly pegged as the guilty party when the lot pointed to him: "And they said every one to his fellow, Come, and let us cast lots, that we may know for whose cause this evil is upon us. So they cast lots, and the lot fell upon Jonah" (Jonah 1:7).

Jonah was tossed overboard and swallowed by a large fish.

In a prophecy about what would happen to Jesus during His life on Earth, the Old Testament predicted that His clothes would be won by gambling: "They part my garments among them, and cast lots upon my vesture" (Psalm 22:18).

The prophecy was fulfilled at the crucifixion of Jesus: "And they crucified him, and parted his garments, casting lots: that it might be fulfilled which was spoken by the prophet, They parted my garments among them, and upon my vesture did they cast lots" (Matthew 27:35).

Shortly after the resurrection of Jesus, the apostles were looking to replace their former colleague, Judas, who had committed suicide after betraying Jesus.

The eleven remaining apostles were undecided about which of two men to select, so they turned to God, using the prayer and lot method.

> And they appointed two, Joseph called Barsabas, who was surnamed Justus, and Matthias. And they prayed, and said, Thou, Lord, which knowest the hearts of all men, shew whether of these two thou hast chosen, that he may take part of this ministry and apostleship, from which Judas by transgression fell, that he might go to his own place. And they gave forth their lots; and the lot fell upon Matthias; and he was numbered with the eleven apostles. (Acts 1:23–26)

The practice of casting lots is certainly biblical. However, before you buy a lottery ticket or book a trip to Vegas, there are other parts of the picture that are important to know. While the Bible contains instances of God's people casting lots, there is no account of a modern lottery with a large cash jackpot. No bingo. No Lotto. No Powerball.

Taking a Chance on God

Does God have a problem with gambling? There is no clear-cut answer. Throughout the Bible, God forbids many specific actions. But not once does He explicitly censure gambling.

The people casting lots in Scripture were only looking to determine the will of God on important issues at hand. The Israelites received their inheritance by casting lots, but they were not placing wagers. There was no chance involved. God directed the outcome, and the Israelites were not taking any risks to get rich. Wherever the lot fell as directed by the Lord, that is where their allotted property would be. The only people who gambled for a prize were the Roman soldiers, with Jesus' clothing going to the winner.

When it comes to playing the lottery today, determining the will of God is not the main reason most people take part. They're looking to get rich quick. The Bible has numerous verses addressing the subject of money, and the desire for instant riches:

> For the love of money is the root of all evil: which while some coveted after, they have erred from the faith, and pierced themselves through with many sorrows. (1 Timothy 6:10)

> Stay away from the love of money; be satisfied with what you have. For God has said, "I will never fail you. I will never forsake you." (Hebrews 13:5 NLT)

> Wealth from get-rich-quick schemes quickly disappears; wealth from hard work grows. (Proverbs 13:11 NLT)

> For riches can disappear as though they had the wings of a bird! (Proverbs 23:5 NLT)

> A greedy person tries to get rich quick, but it only leads to poverty. (Proverbs 28:22 NLT)

> Those who love money will never have enough. How absurd to think that wealth brings true happiness! (Ecclesiastes 5:10 NLT)

> No one can serve two masters. For you will hate one and love the other, or be devoted to one and despise the other. You cannot serve both God and money. (Matthew 6:24 NLT)

As you can see, money and wealth may not be bad in and of themselves, but it's evident that God has a problem with the *love* of money and those who trust in riches. If people are going to put their trust in something, the Bible in many verses says to trust in God. As King David declared in Psalm 56:11: "In God have I put my trust: I will not be afraid what man can do unto me."

CHAPTER TWENTY-TWO

EVERYTHING YOU ALWAYS WANTED TO KNOW ABOUT THE DEVIL BUT WERE AFRAID TO ASK

DID YOU KNOW the Bible calls the devil "god"? That he is known as "the god of this world," while the true God of the universe is never given that title?

Are you aware that the devil is also known as "an angel of light"? That he has a whole army of fellow angels at his disposal? That he and these angels can enter into human beings and take control of their minds and bodies? Did you know the devil was once a guardian of the throne of almighty God before being kicked out of heaven? That he's had to seek permission before inflicting evil?

Our modern world is replete with references to the devil. But you might be astonished to find out what Scripture really has to say about this being.

As we examine the evidence, you will see that the devil is not some rhetorical myth. He is a very real, living, powerful being bent on destroying anything good and godly. Of course, there are those who suggest there is no being known as the devil. They think the term is merely a poetic or literary agent representing evil. Some readers think references to the devil are symbols—fairy-tale figures included to help convey an important message. Others do not believe in any type of spirits, whether referring to God, angels, the devil, or demons. But Scripture paints a very different picture.

The Devil Called "god"

In the King James Version of the Bible, the word *devil* is found sixty-one times in fifty-seven verses. There are also other verses that, though they do not mention the devil by that name, do refer to him as tempter, murderer, accuser, father of lies, god of this world, the prince of the power of the air, serpent, red dragon, Beelzebub (meaning Lord of the flies), and Satan—meaning enemy or adversary—which appears fifty-five times. The Bible apparently has a lot to say about this character.

Perhaps the best place to start is with the high-profile New Testament story in which Jesus Christ of Nazareth, after fasting forty days, was tempted by the devil.

> And Jesus being full of the Holy Ghost returned from Jordan, and was led by the Spirit into the wilderness, being forty days tempted of the devil. And in those days he did eat nothing: and when they were ended, he afterward hungered. And the devil said unto him, If thou be the Son of God, command this stone that it be made bread. And Jesus answered him, saying, It is written, That man shall not live by bread alone, but by every word of God. (Luke 4:1–4)

The text reveals a conversation between two persons out in the wilderness. In sly fashion, the devil used the word *if,* suggesting to Jesus that He was not the Son of God.

Next, he acted as a mode of transportation for Jesus, and disclosed a fascinating piece of information that Jesus did not challenge:

> And the devil, taking him up into an high mountain, shewed unto him all the kingdoms of the world in a moment of time. And the devil said unto him, All this power will I give thee, and the glory of them: for that is delivered unto me; and to whomsoever I will I give it. If thou therefore wilt worship me, all shall be thine. And Jesus answered and said unto him, Get thee behind me, Satan: for it is written, Thou shalt worship the Lord thy God, and him only shalt thou serve. (vv. 5–8)

There are a few interesting points here. First, the devil transported the physically weakened Jesus up to a high mountain. Jesus had just survived forty days without food, so strenuous mountain climbing would not have been on His to-do list. More importantly, Satan made the amazing statement that he himself is the one with power over the kingdoms of the world, and can give that power to whomever he wishes. In none of the accounts of this temptation did Jesus refute that claim. In fact, other New Testament verses agree with the premise that Satan is the one in charge of this present world.

For instance, the apostle Paul specifically referred to Satan as "the god of this world": "But if our gospel be hid, it is hid to them that are lost: in whom the god of this world hath blinded the minds of them which believe not, lest the light of the glorious gospel of Christ, who is the image of God, should shine unto them" (2 Corinthians 4:3–4). Paul was saying that the god of this world, the devil, is blinding the minds of people who do not believe in Jesus Christ.

In similar fashion in John's gospel, Jesus Himself made three references to the devil as "the prince of this world."

Now is the judgment of this world: now shall the prince of this world be cast out. (12:31)

Hereafter I will not talk much with you: for the prince of this world cometh, and hath nothing in me. (14:30)

. . . because the prince of this world is judged. (16:11)

And finally, a note in the New Living Translation for John 12:31 also identifies "the prince of this world" as Satan the devil.

As god of this world, Satan isn't absent from it. Rather, from the very first pages of the Bible to the final book of the New Testament, the devil makes guest appearances.

In Genesis, we find him described as a serpent in the garden of Eden, waiting to utter the first lie ever recorded: "And the serpent said unto the woman, Ye shall not surely die" (3:4). Of course, when Adam and Eve disobeyed God, they ended up dying, instead of living forever as had been intended for them from the beginning.

At the other end of the Bible, Revelation also calls Satan a serpent: "And the great dragon was cast out, that old serpent, called the Devil, and Satan, which deceiveth the whole world: he was cast out into the earth, and his angels were cast out with him" (12:9). This verse is especially helpful in understanding just who or what Satan really is. He is neither man nor God. He is an angel, and not just any angel. The Word of God reveals that Satan was an archangel, the cherub originally assigned to guard the very throne of God, but who was kicked out of heaven for rebelling against God. He is a spirit who dwells both in the unseen world and the physical realm. He and other rebellious angels have the ability to inhabit the minds of people on Earth. According to Scripture, he deceives the whole world.

Satan: The Early Years

Old Testament books such as Ezekiel and Isaiah provide clues about the devil's history. In prophecies regarding the kings of Tyre and Babylon, it's evident that God, speaking through His prophets, was referring not to a human being but to a spirit who at one time lived in heaven, tried to be like the Most High God, was cast out of his glorious home, and ended up in the garden of Eden.

> Son of man, take up a lamentation upon the king of Tyrus, and say unto him, Thus saith the Lord GOD; Thou sealest up the sum, full of wisdom, and perfect in beauty. Thou hast been in Eden the garden of God; every precious stone was thy covering, the sardius, topaz, and the diamond, the beryl, the onyx, and the jasper, the sapphire, the emerald, and the carbuncle, and gold: the workmanship of thy tabrets and of thy pipes was prepared in thee in the day that thou wast created. Thou art the anointed cherub that covereth; and I have set thee so: thou wast upon the holy mountain of God; thou hast walked up and down in the midst of the stones of fire. (Ezekiel 28:12–14)

The NLT renders "the anointed cherub that covereth" as a "guardian": "I ordained and anointed you as the mighty angelic guardian. You had access to the holy mountain of God and walked among the stones of fire" (v. 14).

The king of Tyrus (or Tyre, as we'd say in today's English) was never in Eden; neither was he the anointed cherub that covered God's throne. But Satan was. He began as a brilliant, beautiful angelic creation who resided on the holy mountain of God.

Scripture goes on to use the word *perfect* to describe this person, who, unlike God, was not in existence eternally, but was created at some point in ancient history: "Thou wast perfect in thy ways from the day that thou wast created, till iniquity was found in thee" (v. 15).

And what is iniquity? It is evil, sin, lawlessness, unrighteousness, and perversity. It's anything that goes against the laws or instructions of God.

There are several reasons for Satan's iniquity:

By the multitude of thy merchandise they have filled the midst of thee with violence, and thou hast sinned: therefore I will cast thee as profane out of the mountain of God: and I will destroy thee, O covering cherub, from the midst of the stones of fire. Thine heart was lifted up because of thy beauty, thou hast corrupted thy wisdom by reason of thy brightness. (vv. 16–17)

His beauty led him to become arrogant, his brightness corrupted his wisdom, and he was apparently selling something. Given that he was living in the very throne room of God, it does not make sense that he would be hawking a material product.

Thou hast defiled thy sanctuaries by the multitude of thine iniquities, by the iniquity of thy traffick. (v. 18)

You defiled your sanctuaries with your many sins and your dishonest trade. (NLT)

What specifically might he have been trafficking? What was his "dishonest trade"? If not something physical or material, could it have been an idea? Could it have been rebellion against God? The book of Isaiah provides a few more clues:

How art thou fallen from heaven, O Lucifer, son of the morning! how art thou cut down to the ground, which didst weaken the nations! For thou hast said in thine heart, I will ascend into heaven, I will exalt my throne above the stars of God: I will sit also upon the mount of the congregation, in the sides of the north: I will ascend above the heights of the clouds; I will be like the most High. Yet thou shalt be brought down to hell, to the sides of the pit. (14:12–15)

Lucifer, a Latin name that means light-bearer, initially appeared in the Latin Vulgate version of the Bible some four centuries after Jesus was born. It is not the original word in the Hebrew text. The actual word used in Hebrew is *heylel*, which experts think means something like "shining one."

Here's a modern English version of the same verses:

How you are fallen from heaven, O shining star, son of the morning! You have been thrown down to the earth, you who destroyed the nations of the world. For you said to yourself, "I will ascend to heaven and set my throne above God's stars. I will preside on the mountain of the gods far away in the north. I will climb to the highest heavens and be like the Most High." (vv. 12–14 NLT)

This exceedingly bright archangel who became corrupt had apparently sought to move in on God's territory and establish his own throne in order to "be like the Most High," that is, like God. As a result, he was thrown out of heaven. In fact, Jesus witnessed this unforgettable eviction. He mentioned it during His human ministry, as recorded in Luke's gospel: "And he said unto them, I beheld Satan as lightning fall from heaven" (10:18).

In the New Testament, this aspect of light and brightness remains, especially with the apostle Paul, who wrote that the devil still appears to people as an angel: "Satan himself is transformed into an angel of light" (2 Corinthians 11:14).

When one reads the text surrounding that verse in context, it's clear that Paul was not just warning about Satan, but also about people inspired by the devil who pretend to represent the true God:

For such are false apostles, deceitful workers, transforming themselves into the apostles of Christ. And no marvel; for Satan himself is transformed into an angel of light. Therefore it is no great thing if his ministers also be transformed as the ministers of righteousness; whose end shall be according to their works. (vv. 13–15)

In addition to Satan, there are two other archangels mentioned in the Bible—Michael and Gabriel. Unlike the devil, these two remain faithful to God and are shown to be in an ongoing battle against their former fellow archangel:

And there was war in heaven: Michael and his angels fought against the dragon; and the dragon fought and his angels, and prevailed not; neither was their place found any more in heaven. And the great dragon was cast out, that old serpent, called the Devil, and Satan, which deceiveth the whole world: he was cast out into the earth, and his angels were cast out with him. (Revelation 12:7–9)

This situation is incredible. Satan has his own angels, loyal to him. They apparently agreed with Satan in rebelling against God! There was a massive, galactic conflict waged among angels who chose sides and fought for control of the very dwelling place of the Creator. It was a battle between good and evil far grander than any Hollywood movie.

Satan Wanted Moses' Body

The Bible records another fight between Satan and the archangel Michael as the two were dueling over the dead body of Moses. In just a single verse in the New Testament, we're told there was some kind of dispute over the corpse. "But even Michael, one of the mightiest of the angels, did not dare accuse Satan of blasphemy, but simply said, 'The Lord rebuke you'" (This took place when Michael was arguing with Satan about Moses' body.) (Jude 1:9 NLT).

As bizarre as it sounds, the devil wanted to get his claws on the dead body of the Old Testament prophet Moses. While we're never told why, we can make an educated guess.

Referring back to the time of Moses' actual death, Deuteronomy says:

So Moses the servant of the LORD died there in the land of Moab, according to the word of the LORD. And he buried him in a valley in the land of Moab, over against Bethpeor: but no man knoweth of his sepulchre unto this day. (34:5–6)

According to Scripture, Moses was 120 years old, still full of strength and with excellent eyesight. He passed away in the land of Moab, as God did not allow him to enter the promised land with the rest of the Israelites. But his body was not buried by his fellow Israelites. God was the one who took care of the interment, and no human being ever knew the precise location of the tomb. Obviously, God had a reason for personally handling his burial.

The Israelites were notorious for worshipping objects other than the true God. They made a calf of gold to worship just days after being freed from their captivity in Egypt. They were quick to turn to the pagan customs of nations around them and set their hearts on anything other than the real God of the universe. Had Moses' burial place become known, it's possible the site itself would have become an object of worship.

The devil looks for any way he can to cause people to focus their attention on something or someone other than God. In this case, it seems plausible that the devil was looking to disclose where the body of Moses lay so people would worship it.

Speak of the Devil

When the devil speaks, he certainly cannot be trusted. Jesus said the devil does not have any truth in him, even calling him the "father" of lies:

Ye are of your father the devil, and the lusts of your father ye will do. He was a murderer from the beginning, and abode not in the truth, because there is no truth in him. When he speaketh a lie, he speaketh of his own: for he is a liar, and the father of it. (John 8:44)

Satan still speaks with God, and interestingly, there are times when he needs permission to wreak havoc. For example, in the book of Job, Satan is presented as not only traveling globally but as having access to God's dwelling place in heaven.

Now there was a day when the sons of God came to present themselves before the LORD, and Satan came also among them. And the LORD said unto Satan, Whence comest thou? Then Satan answered the LORD, and said, From going to and fro in the earth, and from walking up and down in it. (1:6–7)

God asked Satan if he had observed a man named Job, who was faithful in all his ways. In reply, Satan suggested that Job was only obedient because he had experienced a multitude of blessings from God, including good health and wealth. God then granted Satan permission to test Job, allowing the devil to strike the man with a series of personal calamities that made his life miserable. "And the LORD said unto Satan, Behold, all that he hath is in thy power; only upon himself put not forth thine hand. So Satan went forth from the presence of the LORD" (v. 12).

Despite sudden disaster in his life, Job refused to sin by cursing God. So Satan returned to ask permission to afflict Job personally with diseases, and again, God gave him the green light. "But put forth thine hand now, and touch his bone and his flesh, and he will curse thee to thy face. And the LORD said unto Satan, Behold, he is in thine hand; but save his life" (2:5–6).

While the Bible does not reveal other detailed scenarios in which Satan had to seek permission to strike someone, the inclusion of this account certainly raises the possibility that the devil might require approval from God before taking action in any circumstance.

The Devil Made Him Do It

For much of the remainder of the Bible, the devil and his angels, who are referred to as "devils" and "demons," do their dirty work here on Earth. They try to influence people to make choices contrary to God's will, beginning with Eve in the garden. In the New Testament gospels, these fallen angels take up residence inside the minds and bodies of human beings. Sometimes even more than one spirit lives inside a person, as we read in Luke, "And Jesus asked him, saying, What is thy name? And he said, Legion: because many devils were entered into him" (8:30).

On the night of the Last Supper, before Jesus was crucified, Satan personally possessed Judas, the apostle who betrayed Jesus.

Then entered Satan into Judas surnamed Iscariot, being of the number of the twelve. (Luke 22:3)

As soon as Judas had eaten the bread, Satan entered into him. Then Jesus told him, "Hurry. Do it now." (John 13:27 NLT)

When the devil and his angels possess people, they can cause the "host human" great physical harm. In one instance, a demon-possessed boy continually threw himself into fire and water. While the apostles were unable to exorcise the demon, Jesus accomplished the task. Here is how Mark records the event:

> When Jesus saw that the people came running together, he rebuked the foul spirit, saying unto him, Thou dumb and deaf spirit, I charge thee, come out of him, and enter no more into him. And the spirit cried, and rent him sore, and came out of him: and he was as one dead; insomuch that many said, He is dead. But Jesus took him by the hand, and lifted him up; and he arose. And when he was come into the house, his disciples asked him privately, Why could not we cast him out? And he said unto them, This kind can come forth by nothing, but by prayer and fasting. (9:25–29)

In Matthew's version of the same exorcism, an additional comment from Jesus reveals that a lack of faith prevented the disciples from removing the demon.

> And Jesus said unto them, Because of your unbelief: for verily I say unto you, If ye have faith as a grain of mustard seed, ye shall say unto this mountain, Remove hence to yonder place; and it shall remove; and nothing shall be impossible unto you. (17:20)

The devil and demons are not mythical figures. They are every bit as real as God. Just because they usually do not appear visibly does not nullify their existence. They dwell among the human populace, unseen to the naked eye but present nonetheless.

In summary, the devil is a powerful spirit created long before men and women were ever put on this planet. He is a formerly high-ranking angel—albeit an enigmatic, rebellious one—who is now called "the god of this world." He has had conversations with God, both in heaven and here on Earth, has led his own army of fallen angels in battle against God's faithful angels, and is doing his worst, so to speak, to deceive the world away from worship of the true God in order for himself to be worshipped as God.

When it comes to evil, the Bible makes it clear Satan is the true Public Enemy number one:

> Be sober, be vigilant; because your adversary the devil, as a roaring lion, walketh about, seeking whom he may devour. (1 Peter 5:8)

CHAPTER TWENTY-THREE

HARRY POTTER AND THE WRATH OF GOD

EVERYONE'S JUST WILD about Harry—Harry Potter, that is. The famous character has created a worldwide sensation.

Harry Potter is a fictional boy wizard created by author J. K. Rowling. Harry's magical exploits have captivated children across the globe, casting what appears to be a worldwide spell on young minds. The Harry Potter series has been translated into many languages, and the stories have hit the silver screen as motion-picture blockbusters.

With fans lining up for each new book in the series, and theaters packed, there's no doubt the franchise is a literary juggernaut.

God Spells It Out

Harry Potter, of course, is not mentioned in the Bible. But Scripture does have quite a bit to say about witches, wizards, sorcery, and virtually anything to do with the occult. For instance, Leviticus has simple, straightforward instructions: "Do not practice fortune-telling or witchcraft . . . Do not rely on mediums and psychics, for you will be defiled by them" (19:26, 31 NLT).

The book of Exodus calls for the death penalty for those engaged in witchcraft: "A sorceress must not be allowed to live" (22:18 NLT).

The Bible lists many aspects of the occult, from casting spells and telling fortunes to seeking communication with the dead:

And do not let your people practice fortune-telling or sorcery, or allow them to interpret omens, or engage in witchcraft, or cast spells, or function as mediums or psychics, or call forth the spirits of the dead. Anyone who does these things is an object of horror and disgust to the LORD. (Deuteronomy 18:10–12 NLT)

The King James Version of these verses actually uses the term *wizard* in its listing.

Many people today have a strong interest in astrology, believing that the positions and movements of planets and stars have a profound impact on world events and the character traits with which people are born. They read their horoscopes in the newspaper each day. "What's your sign?" was a popular catchphrase in the 1970s, as people seeking compatibility sought to discover someone else's zodiac sign. But the Bible is not silent about putting one's trust in celestial bodies:

And when you look up into the sky and see the sun, moon, and stars—all the forces of heaven—don't be seduced by them and worship them. The LORD your God designated these heavenly bodies for all the peoples of the earth. (Deuteronomy 4:19 NLT)

Suppose a man or woman among you, in one of your towns that the LORD your God is giving you, has done evil in the sight of the LORD your God and has violated the covenant by serving other gods or by worshiping the sun, the moon, or any of the forces of heaven, which I have strictly forbidden. When you hear about it, investigate the matter thoroughly. If it is true that this detestable thing has been done in Israel, then that man or woman must be taken to the gates of the town and stoned to death. (Deuteronomy 17:2–5 NLT)

After the kingdom of ancient Israel split into two separate kingdoms, Manasseh ruled the Southern Kingdom of Judah. The book of 2 Chronicles has a laundry list of the evils he committed, with occult-related activity featured prominently.

Manasseh even sacrificed his own sons in the fire in the valley of the son of Hinnom. He practiced sorcery, divination, and witchcraft, and he

consulted with mediums and psychics. He did much that was evil in the
LORD's sight, arousing his anger. (33:6 NLT)

God's warning against the occult is not limited to the Old Testament, as
witchcraft is listed among other sins in the New Testament. The apostle Paul
said that people who engage in it will not inherit the kingdom of God.

Now the works of the flesh are manifest, which are these; Adultery, fornication, uncleanness, lasciviousness, idolatry, witchcraft, . . . and such
like: of the which I tell you before, as I have also told you in time past,
that they which do such things shall not inherit the kingdom of God.
(Galatians 5:19–21)

Also, the book of Revelation predicts that witchcraft will continue to be
practiced to the end of this present age leading up to the return of Jesus
Christ: "And they did not repent of their murders or their witchcraft or their
immorality or their thefts" (9:21 NLT).

While the world is just wild about Harry, the Bible makes it clear that
God has a problem with Harry's craft of wizardry and wants people to stay
far away from it. Witches, wizards, psychics, and sorcerers are not cute and
harmless in the eyes of God. Scripture says God finds them disgusting, and
people engaged in the occult will not inherit the kingdom of God.

CHAPTER TWENTY-FOUR

FOR SALE: THE HOLY SPIRIT?

NEARLY EVERYONE these days buys or sells on eBay, and sometimes the items up for bid can get a little strange.

In 2005, a Pennsylvania man sold a stain on his shower tile that he said looked like the face of Jesus. "Shower Jesus has been freed from the wall!" his ad proclaimed, as he hawked "a section of plaster wall bearing the apparent face of the Son of God. No other items, promises, tidings, or guarantees are included." A bidder eventually bought the item for just under two thousand dollars.

Long before eBay existed, the Bible told an interesting tale of an actual attempt to purchase the Holy Spirit of God! The story is found in the book of Acts, as readers are introduced to a well-known magician.

> A man named Simon had been a sorcerer there for many years, claiming to be someone great. The Samaritan people, from the least to the greatest, often spoke of him as "the Great One—the Power of God." He was very influential because of the magic he performed. (8:9–11 NLT)

Given his skill in sorcery, Simon probably did not expect to find a power greater than his own. However, the power of God bedazzled him to such an extent that he became a believer.

> But now the people believed Philip's message of Good News concerning

the Kingdom of God and the name of Jesus Christ. As a result, many men and women were baptized. Then Simon himself believed and was baptized. He began following Philip wherever he went, and he was amazed by the great miracles and signs Philip performed. (vv. 12–13 NLT)

Philip was a believer full of the Holy Spirit and thus able to perform miracles, but according to the text, new converts to Christianity did not have this ability, since they did not have the Spirit.

When the apostles back in Jerusalem heard that the people of Samaria had accepted God's message, they sent Peter and John there. As soon as they arrived, they prayed for these new Christians to receive the Holy Spirit. The Holy Spirit had not yet come upon any of them, for they had only been baptized in the name of the Lord Jesus. (vv. 14–16 NLT)

When Jesus' apostles Peter and John arrived, Simon grew even more amazed as he saw how the Spirit was given to the new believers through the laying on of hands. Then his thoughts turned to cash and purchasing the power of God.

Then Peter and John laid their hands upon these believers, and they received the Holy Spirit. When Simon saw that the Holy Spirit was given when the apostles placed their hands upon people's heads, he offered money to buy this power. "Let me have this power, too," he exclaimed, "so that when I lay my hands on people, they will receive the Holy Spirit!" (vv. 17–19 NLT)

Simon was a new believer in Jesus, and he obviously did not realize the problem with his offer. He almost certainly didn't expect such a scathing response from Peter, who spared nothing in thrashing Simon for his line of thought.

But Peter replied, "May your money perish with you for thinking God's gift can be bought! You can have no part in this, for your heart is not right before God. Turn from your wickedness and pray to the Lord. Perhaps he will forgive your evil thoughts, for I can see that you are full of bitterness and held captive by sin." (vv. 20–23 NLT)

The rebuke apparently stung Simon, as the final line in the story notes a personal plea to spare him from calamity. "'Pray to the Lord for me,' Simon exclaimed, 'that these terrible things won't happen to me!'" (v. 24 NLT).

The modern word *simony*, meaning the buying or selling of sacred or spiritual things, originated with this single incident.

To make it clear to all those speculators and investors out there, even though Shower Jesus could be purchased, the Holy Spirit is not for sale at any price.

CHAPTER TWENTY-FIVE

DAZE OF OUR WIVES

DID YOU KNOW that a nagging wife is like the sound of a constant dripping? I did not make that up. It comes directly from the Holy Bible, which has plenty to say on the subject of wives and marriage, both good and bad.

Starting with the good, Scripture indicates:

> Whoso findeth a wife findeth a good thing, and obtaineth favour of the LORD. (Proverbs 18:22)

> A prudent wife is from the LORD. (Proverbs 19:14)

> A worthy wife is her husband's joy and crown. (Proverbs 12:4 NLT)

> Who can find a virtuous and capable wife? She is worth more than precious rubies. (Proverbs 31:10 NLT)

The Bible is clear that there's something wonderful about a good woman who can help a man be his best. However, not all women are the same, and certainly not every woman is esteemed like precious jewels.

King Solomon, author of the book of Proverbs, who was infused by God with wisdom, had a few choice thoughts about women who today might be known as "henpeckers."

A nagging wife annoys like a constant dripping. (Proverbs 19:13 NLT)

It is better to dwell in a corner of the housetop, than with a brawling woman in a wide house. (Proverbs 21:9)

It is better to live alone in the desert than with a crabby, complaining wife. (Proverbs 21:19 NLT)

Maybe Solomon had too much of a good thing, as we're told in 1 Kings 11:3, "And he had seven hundred wives, princesses, and three hundred concubines."

When God Mandated Divorce

Are you aware that God once ordered more than one hundred of His people to end their marriages, and that it had nothing to do with nagging? It's true. God ordered a bunch of married people, even those with children, to split up. (If divorce lawyers had been around in biblical times, they could have made a killing!)

The divorces were mandated despite the fact that God is the number one advocate for marriage and strong family ties. In fact, it was God Himself who presented the first woman, Eve, to the first man, Adam. In Genesis 2:25, God called the couple "the man and his wife," and earlier instructed them to "be fruitful, and multiply" (Genesis 1:28). God, of course, is a family, even using family names such as Father and Son, and refers to human beings who are obedient as the children of God.

And God is certainly no big fan of divorce. He even says He hates it:

You cry out, "Why has the LORD abandoned us?" I'll tell you why! Because the LORD witnessed the vows you and your wife made to each other on your wedding day when you were young. But you have been disloyal to her, though she remained your faithful companion, the wife of your marriage vows.

Didn't the LORD make you one with your wife? In body and spirit you are his. And what does he want? Godly children from your union. So guard yourself; remain loyal to the wife of your youth. "For I hate divorce!" says the LORD, the God of Israel. "It is as cruel as putting on a

victim's bloodstained coat," says the LORD Almighty. "So guard yourself;
always remain loyal to your wife." (Malachi 2:14–16 NLT)

In the New Testament, Jesus reiterated the anti-divorce theme when He
stated, "What therefore God hath joined together, let not man put asunder"
(Matthew 19:6).

But despite God being pro-marriage and anti-divorce, more than one
hundred men were told to leave not only their wives but also any children
they had.

The mandatory divorce order was issued because the men had married
the wrong kind of women. That did not mean they slept around, used foul
language, gossiped about town, did not use enough deodorant, or left the
toothpaste cap off the tube.

Instead, these women were pagans, who either worshipped other gods or
kept heathen traditions associated with those nonexistent gods.

The story is tucked away in the last two chapters of the book of Ezra.

Ezra was a priest some five hundred years before the birth of Jesus. He
was one of the men who led a remnant of God's people out of Babylonian
captivity and back to Jerusalem to rebuild the temple and reinstitute the
ways of God. While some decided to stay in Babylon, others eagerly sought
to return to their ancestral homeland and establish a lifestyle under God's
instruction, this time without the paganism.

Ezra wrote in the first person to describe some shocking news he
received.

But then the Jewish leaders came to me and said, "Many of the people of
Israel, and even some of the priests and Levites, have not kept themselves
separate from the other peoples living in the land. They have taken up
the detestable practices of the Canaanites, Hittites, Perizzites, Jebusites,
Ammonites, Moabites, Egyptians, and Amorites. For the men of Israel
have married women from these people and have taken them as wives for
their sons. So the holy race has become polluted by these mixed marriages. To make matters worse, the officials and leaders are some of the
worst offenders." (Ezra 9:1–2 NLT)

Ezra was so stunned to learn of the marriages to pagan women that he
tore his clothes and began yanking chunks of hair out of his head and beard:

"When I heard this, I tore my clothing, pulled hair from my head and beard, and sat down utterly shocked" (v. 3 NLT).

Ezra did not know what to do or where to turn, except to God. He offered up a public prayer, admitting that he was ashamed to inform the Lord of the people's mixed marriages.

> And now, O our God, what shall we say after this? for we have forsaken thy commandments, which thou hast commanded by thy servants the prophets, saying, The land, unto which ye go to possess it, is an unclean land with the filthiness of the people of the lands, with their abominations, which have filled it from one end to another with their uncleanness. Now therefore give not your daughters unto their sons, neither take their daughters unto your sons, nor seek their peace or their wealth for ever: that ye may be strong, and eat the good of the land, and leave it for an inheritance to your children for ever . . . Should we again break thy commandments, and join in affinity with the people of these abominations? (vv. 10–12, 14)

During the course of his prayer, Ezra was surrounded by a large crowd of men, women, and children who heard his plea, and they all wept bitterly for their transgression. Finally, one of the repentant men approached Ezra with the solution:

> Then Shecaniah son of Jehiel, a descendant of Elam, said to Ezra, "We confess that we have been unfaithful to our God, for we have married these pagan women of the land. But there is hope for Israel in spite of this. Let us now make a covenant with our God to divorce our pagan wives and to send them away with their children. We will follow the advice given by you and by the others who respect the commands of our God. We will obey the law of God. (10:2–3 NLT)

After three days of continued prayer and complete fasting (no food or water), Ezra issued the order to split the families, saying it came from God: "Confess your sin to the LORD, the God of your ancestors, and do what he demands. Separate yourselves from the people of the land and from these pagan women" (v. 11 NLT).

The congregation agreed with a loud voice, and they sought to dissolve the marriages in a calm, orderly fashion. The matter was investigated for three months to determine precisely who was guilty of marrying someone who was not a descendant of Israel. The total came to 111 men, who subsequently broke off their marriages, even if they had children.

Peter and the Wife

Today, some two thousand years after Jesus of Nazareth walked the Earth as a human, there is a rampant misconception about the apostle Simon Peter. Many people think Peter never got married or had sex with a wife. But the gospels of Matthew, Mark, and Luke all make clear that Peter did indeed have a wife.

The accounts never actually mention the name of Mrs. Peter, but they do make note of the miraculous healing of Peter's mother-in-law. Here is the account from each of the Gospels.

> When Jesus arrived at Peter's house, Peter's mother-in-law was in bed with a high fever. But when Jesus touched her hand, the fever left her. Then she got up and prepared a meal for him. (Matthew 8:14–15 NLT)

> And forthwith, when they were come out of the synagogue, they entered into the house of Simon and Andrew, with James and John. But Simon's wife's mother lay sick of a fever, and anon they tell him of her. And he came and took her by the hand, and lifted her up; and immediately the fever left her, and she ministered unto them. (Mark 1:29–31)

> And he arose out of the synagogue, and entered into Simon's house. And Simon's wife's mother was taken with a great fever; and they besought him for her. And he stood over her, and rebuked the fever; and it left her: and immediately she arose and ministered unto them. (Luke 4:38–39)

Obviously, Simon Peter could not have had a "wife's mother" or "mother-in-law" unless he'd had a wife!

Perhaps part of the reason the legend of Peter's eternal bachelorhood has survived over the years is that Jesus Himself was never married. For those in the Roman Catholic faith especially, Peter is regarded as the first pope. Since Catholic priests and popes take vows of celibacy today, it's easy to see why some may assume Peter was also celibate. But the Bible says differently. Peter did have a wife. And we can only hope her name was not "Constance Dripping."

CHAPTER TWENTY-SIX

NOAH, ABRAHAM, ISAAC, AND JACOB WERE NOT JEWS

HERE'S A NEWSFLASH! Some of the biggest names mentioned in the Old Testament were not Jews. You read that right, not Jews.

Adam was not Jewish; neither was his wife, Eve, or their sons, Cain, Abel, and Seth. Noah was not a Jew. What may be more astonishing to some is the fact that Abraham, Isaac, and even Jacob—the man whose name became Israel—were not Jews either.

While most people think the Jews are the focus of the Old Testament, according to the Bible, they are not. This does not mean there are no Jews found in the Old Testament. There certainly are. But one of the most prevalent misconceptions about Scripture is that the Old Testament centers only on Jews and Judaism, while the New Testament focuses on Christians and Christianity.

The first mention of the word *Jews* does not appear until deep within Scripture. Scour through Genesis, Exodus, Leviticus, Numbers, and Deuteronomy, and you will come up empty. Mine the next five books, and still you come up with nothing. The first time the word is even found in the King James Version is twelve books into the Bible, in 2 Kings, many centuries after human beings had been created by God. Here is the verse: "At that time Rezin king of Syria recovered Elath to Syria, and drave the Jews from Elath: and the Syrians came to Elath, and dwelt there unto this day" (16:6).

To understand why many of the well-known personalities of the Old Testament were not Jews or Jewish, we have to go back to the beginning. In Genesis, there is no mention that God was creating "Jews." The text says He created humankind in two genders: "So God created man in his own image, in the image of God created he him; male and female created he them" (1:27).

For centuries after this initial creation, there was not even a hint of someone being Jewish. Thus, sons and daughters of Adam and Eve were not Jewish. Righteous followers of God, such as Enoch, were not Jews. Likewise, those who did not follow the teachings of God were not Jews either.

Even the patriarchs of modern-day Judaism—men such as Abraham, Isaac, and Jacob—were not Jews! It may sound incredible, but it's true. There was no religion in Abraham's day called Judaism. Neither was there a single person at that time that was of Jewish ethnicity or of the Jewish faith.

The word *Jews* derives from the word *Judah*, the name of one of the great-grandsons of Abraham. Here is his story:

Abraham had a son named Isaac, and Isaac had a son named Jacob. After struggling with God, Jacob was given a new name, Israel. That name does *not* mean Jew or Jewish. It simply means "one who struggles with God and prevails" or "prince with God."

Israel had twelve sons, one of whom he named Judah, meaning "praise." His birth by his mother, Leah, is recorded in Genesis: "And she conceived again, and bare a son: and she said, Now will I praise the LORD: therefore she called his name Judah; and left bearing" (29:35). Again, it is this Old Testament person who is the origin of the name Jew. The names of his eleven brothers were Reuben, Simeon, Levi, Dan, Naphtali, Gad, Asher, Isaachar, Zebulun, Joseph, and Benjamin.

To give a quick historical overview, all twelve sons of Israel, including Judah, traveled into Egypt to escape a great famine in their own land. Hundreds of years later, the descendants of these twelve sons, the twelve "tribes" of Israel, all became oppressed as slaves in Egypt after a new leader had risen to power. Moses, who was not a descendant of Judah, led the people out of Egypt. He brought them to the brink of the promised land, which was the land where Abraham, Isaac, and Jacob had lived half a century previously.

The descendants of Israel had multiplied greatly by the time they moved into the promised land, but each tribe of Israel still went by its own name, and families received land according to the tribes of their birth. For instance, the descendants of Reuben received a portion of land in one region. Descendants of Dan received another allotment. The sons of Judah received their own portion as well.

Years passed, and the Israelites, like the pagan nations, demanded a king to rule over them. God reluctantly agreed to the demand for a king, and appointed a man named Saul, who hailed from the tribe of Benjamin. But Saul quickly fell out of favor with God, and a new king, who happened to be a descendant of Judah, was anointed by God as Saul's successor. That man was David, who as a young man slew Goliath with a stone and slingshot. David, who was called a "man after God's own heart," ascended to great power as the king over the united kingdom of Israel, with all twelve tribes subject to his sovereignty.

Following David's death, the rulership of the land fell upon his son, Solomon. The Bible says Solomon "was wiser than all men," but toward the end of his life, he allowed his numerous pagan wives to influence his adherence to God's laws. This was a key factor that led to major trouble for the kingdom. In fact, it led to its fracture.

And the LORD was angry with Solomon, because his heart was turned from the LORD God of Israel, which had appeared unto him twice, and had commanded him concerning this thing, that he should not go after other gods: but he kept not that which the LORD commanded. Wherefore the LORD said unto Solomon, Forasmuch as this is done of thee, and thou hast not kept my covenant and my statutes, which I have commanded thee, I will surely rend the kingdom from thee, and will give it to thy servant. Notwithstanding in thy days I will not do it for David thy father's sake: but I will rend it out of the hand of thy son. (1 Kings 11:9–12)

The prophecy came true, and the united kingdom of Israel was split into two kingdoms. If you have not already figured it out by now, the kingdoms were named the "kingdom of Israel" and the "kingdom of Judah." Israel became a ten-tribe group in the northern part of the territory. In the southern region, Judah was actually made up of three tribes—Judah, Benjamin, and Levi, all of whom collectively became known as "Jews." The total adds up to thirteen because the tribe of Joseph was given a double portion as a special blessing. The names of those tribes were Ephraim and Manasseh, the two sons of Joseph.

Thus, what was once a single kingdom of all the tribes of Israel became two kingdoms. It was the citizens living in the kingdom of Judah who bore the name "Jews." Throughout the Old Testament books of Kings and Chronicles, one can see the names of the kings of both kingdoms, as the people experienced both godly leaders and ungodly ones.

Like the North and South during the U.S. Civil War, at times Israel was actually at war with the Jews! That may seem inconceivable to people who are under the impression that the people of Israel and Jews are one and the same. That takes us back to the first mention of the word *Jews*. Ironically, the initial instance of the word *Jews* in the Bible is the very time when Israel was at war with the Jews.

> Then Rezin king of Syria and Pekah son of Remaliah king of Israel came up to Jerusalem to war: and they besieged Ahaz, but could not overcome him. At that time Rezin king of Syria recovered Elath to Syria, and drave the Jews from Elath: and the Syrians came to Elath, and dwelt there unto this day. (2 Kings 16:5–6)

The citizens of Israel, whose king at the time was Remaliah, went to war against the Jews of the kingdom of Judah, whose king was Ahaz. At the very first indication of Jews, we find that Israel is not synonymous with Jews. It was in conflict with them. While the citizens of the Southern Kingdom become known as the people of Judah, or Jews, their northern cousins retained the name Israel. Eventually, both kingdoms fell under attack to different foreign nations; Israel fell victim to the Assyrians in 721 BC, and Judah was invaded by the Babylonians in 586 BC.

The Northern Kingdom of Israel never returned to its rightful land, and became known as the lost ten tribes of Israel. The Jews, however, did return to Jerusalem after their Babylonian captivity. That's why by the time Jesus was born, the land was once again filled with Jews, and the region was known as Judaea, not Israel.

The difference between the terms *Israelite* and *Jew* is more easily understood when compared to the United States today. While it's fair to say that all legal citizens of Nebraska are Americans, certainly not all Americans are Nebraskans. There are forty-nine other states of which they could be citizens.

In the same way, while all Jews were Israelites since they descended from Judah, the son of Israel, not all Israelites were Jews. Israelites may have belonged to one of several other tribes.

You know that chicken wings can't exist without chickens. Likewise, there's no apple cider without apples, and no banana cream pie without bananas. Thus, fundamentally, there cannot be Jews without Judah existing first. Until there was even a person who had the name of Judah, everyone born before him could not possibly be a Jew. Therefore, Noah, Abraham, Isaac, and Jacob, along with everyone else who was alive before Judah, could not have been Jews, which seriously calls into question the notion that Jews are the focus of the Old Testament.

CHAPTER TWENTY-SEVEN

PAGE-TWO MIRACLES

MOST EVERYONE KNOWS about the famous, front-page miracles of the Bible, such as the parting of the Red Sea, Jesus turning water into wine, or Jesus being raised from the dead. But the Bible is a book loaded with extraordinary events, many of which never receive the attention they deserve. In the spirit of correcting that error, here are a few incredible items you may have never heard of or may have forgotten about.

The Other Guy Walking on Water

One of the most famous events of the New Testament took place when Jesus of Nazareth walked on water. Even today, if someone asks a person on the street to name one of Jesus' miracles, walking on water will probably be among them. In fact, many now equate the phrase "walking on water" with supernatural ability.

But many do not know that Jesus was not the *only* person to walk on water. There was another man who did the same thing.

So who is it? Peter, a fisherman chosen to be an apostle of Jesus. The event is recounted in the same story where Jesus marched atop the sea, in Matthew 14.

But the ship was now in the midst of the sea, tossed with waves: for the wind was contrary. And in the fourth watch of the night Jesus went unto them, walking on the sea. And when the disciples saw him walking on the sea, they were troubled, saying, It is a spirit; and they cried out for fear. But straightway Jesus spake unto them, saying, Be of good cheer; it is I; be not afraid. And Peter answered him and said, Lord, if it be thou, bid me come unto thee on the water. And he said, Come. And when Peter was come down out of the ship, he walked on the water, to go to Jesus. But when he saw the wind boisterous, he was afraid; and beginning to sink, he cried, saying, Lord, save me. And immediately Jesus stretched forth his hand, and caught him, and said unto him, O thou of little faith, wherefore didst thou doubt? And when they were come into the ship, the wind ceased. Then they that were in the ship came and worshipped him, saying, Of a truth thou art the Son of God. (vv. 24–33)

The more you read this passage, the more interesting it becomes. A boatload of tough-guy fishermen were freaking out because they thought they were seeing a spirit doing the impossible—walking on top of water without sinking!

But it's not as though they hadn't seen miracles before. They had experienced many. In fact, this event came hours after Jesus took five loaves of bread and two fishes and fed some five thousand men, not counting the women and children in the crowd.

Peter was not sure it was Jesus he was seeing on the water until Jesus identified Himself and told Peter to get out of the boat and come closer. The vessel was not close to shore where the two could have been wading. It was "in the midst of the sea."

"And when Peter was come down out of the ship, he walked on the water, to go to Jesus."

There is no way around it; the Bible says Peter was doing the impossible and walking on water. The report does not say exactly how far he walked on the surface. It may have been a few steps or twenty yards. But it does note that when doubt began to enter Peter's mind, he started to sink. When he cried out to be saved, Jesus was there to catch him.

It's also interesting to note Jesus' attitude toward his friend. If someone today were involved in a rescue at sea, they might be concerned for the rescued person's welfare and feelings of security.

Jesus, however, had a different strategy. He was miffed at Peter, blasting him as someone with "little faith" and wondering why he doubted after experiencing all those earlier miracles, including having just walked on water!

What are some other underreported miracles in the Bible?

Long-Distance Exorcise

If you think you live a busy life, consider how it was for God's apostles in the fledgling days of Christianity. So many people wanted to be healed, yet there was so little time to get around to them all—especially since the automobile was still some nineteen centuries away.

So what was done when someone needed a demon kicked out of him, and the exorcist was too busy? The Bible describes a solution, at least for some people. It mentions briefly that the apostle Paul did not have to be present in order to work miracles: "God gave Paul the power to do unusual miracles, so that even when handkerchiefs or cloths that had touched his skin were placed on sick people, they were healed of their diseases, and any evil spirits within them came out" (Acts 19:11–12 NLT).

Not only did Paul have the power to heal people of their sicknesses and exorcise demons, but Scripture says he could do it long-distance by having something that he wore or a cloth that touched his skin come in contact with the person in need. He handled exorcisms by proxy. This special ability of Paul gives new meaning to the expression *man of the cloth*.

Venom That Couldn't Kill

Imagine you're on a voyage, traveling to a destination far from the safety and comfort of your own home. The weather turns nasty, bringing pounding rains, fierce winds, and bone-chilling temperatures. Conditions are harsh, and it soon becomes obvious you're in trouble. Your vessel is losing its integrity and will shortly become a shipwreck statistic.

The boat finally breaks apart, and you and your shipmates are swimming for your lives. Finally you make it to shore, with the rain still hammering and the mercury dropping. Just as you begin to catch your breath and someone builds a fire to keep warm, a poisonous snake slithers out and latches on to your hand, pumping lethal venom into your bloodstream. What would you do? Tear the serpent from your limb and suck out the venom? Scream for help? *Soil yourself?*

How about doing nothing and ignoring the threat completely?

Such a scenario occurred in the New Testament, with the apostle Paul as the victim of both a shipwreck and subsequent snake attack. But Paul didn't panic, and he certainly didn't mess himself. The events are recorded in the twenty-seventh and twenty-eighth chapters of the book of Acts.

While others were fretting over the life-threatening nature of the storm, Paul had good reason to know both he and his shipmates would be safe. He was told as much by an angel who made a personal appearance to him, and he relayed this information to the 275 others on board with him.

> And now I exhort you to be of good cheer: for there shall be no loss of any man's life among you, but of the ship. For there stood by me this night the angel of God, whose I am, and whom I serve, saying, Fear not, Paul; thou must be brought before Caesar: and, lo, God hath given thee all them that sail with thee. Wherefore, sirs, be of good cheer: for I believe God, that it shall be even as it was told me. (27:22–25)

When Paul's ship finally struck ground and began disintegrating, some Roman soldiers suggested that the prisoners—including Paul—should be slaughtered immediately so they could not swim ashore and escape. However, a commanding officer, who sought to spare Paul, rejected the idea.

> But the centurion, willing to save Paul, kept them from their purpose; and commanded that they which could swim should cast themselves first into the sea, and get to land: and the rest, some on boards, and some on broken pieces of the ship. And so it came to pass, that they escaped all safe to land. (vv. 43–44)

Paul and the others had arrived alive on the island of Malta. But then, in the fashion of a modern-day horror flick, the danger kept coming, even while the survivors sought shelter.

> The people of the island were very kind to us. It was cold and rainy, so they built a fire on the shore to welcome us and warm us. As Paul gathered an armful of sticks and was laying them on the fire, a poisonous snake, driven out by the heat, fastened itself onto his hand. The people of the island saw it hanging there and said to each other, "A murderer, no

doubt! Though he escaped the sea, justice will not permit him to live." But Paul shook off the snake into the fire and was unharmed. The people waited for him to swell up or suddenly drop dead. But when they had waited a long time and saw no harm come to him, they changed their minds and decided he was a god. (28:2–6 NLT)

What a powerful statement of faith. Despite the fact a viper had just sunk its teeth into Paul's hand, the apostle did not appear startled. He shook it off into the fire as if it never happened. The locals of Malta were amazed, as they had initially thought Paul must have been a convicted killer, and the snake was sent as some kind of divine retribution.

As they anxiously waited for Paul's impending death, all eyes were focused on this mysterious man who had survived both the shipwreck and the swim to shore. Would he also survive a bite from a dangerous viper?

The Scriptures say he did. And when it became clear that Paul was unharmed, it's hardly surprising that these pagan worshippers jumped to the erroneous conclusion Paul was a god.

The Biggest Freaking Night-Light in History

Why doesn't God plainly show Himself? This is a common sentiment among both believers and nonbelievers. Many think, *If only there were some unmistakable evidence of a higher power, then my faith would be unwavering.* After all, seeing is believing.

Yet one of the longest-lasting and underreported miracles in biblical history suggests that no matter how often God makes Himself visible, seeing is *not* believing. Worse, regardless of how many times God allows people to witness His power and glory, they will still continue to rebel.

I am referring to God's four-decade appearance as a giant, pillar-shaped cloud during daylight hours, and a pillar of blazing fire at night. Beginning at the time of the Exodus from Egypt, God manifested Himself as a massive pillar stretching perhaps from the sky to the earth, leading the Israelites on their journey.

And the LORD went before them by day in a pillar of a cloud, to lead them the way; and by night in a pillar of fire, to give them light; to go by day and night: He took not away the pillar of the cloud by day, nor the pillar of fire by night, from before the people. (Exodus 13:21–22)

When the Egyptians, after releasing the Israelites, changed their minds and pursued them into the wilderness, they encountered God in the form of this pillar.

> And the angel of God, which went before the camp of Israel, removed and went behind them; and the pillar of the cloud went from before their face, and stood behind them: and it came between the camp of the Egyptians and the camp of Israel; and it was a cloud and darkness to them, but it gave light by night to these: so that the one came not near the other all the night. (Exodus 14:19–20)

God, while appearing both as a pillar of cloud and a pillar of fire, became an agent of protection for His people. From the vanguard position in front, He moved to the rear, positioning Himself between the Israelites and the oncoming Egyptians. And not only was the pillar a dividing wall; it created darkness for the Egyptians and light for the Israelites moments before the magnificent splitting of the Red Sea.

The pillar was also a daily travel guide, as the people would move their camp only when the cloud would rise up and move in a given direction.

> This was the regular pattern—at night the cloud changed to the appearance of fire. When the cloud lifted from over the sacred tent, the people of Israel followed it. And wherever the cloud settled, the people of Israel camped. In this way, they traveled at the LORD's command and stopped wherever he told them to. Then they remained where they were as long as the cloud stayed over the Tabernacle . . . Sometimes the cloud stayed only overnight and moved on the next morning. But day or night, when the cloud lifted, the people broke camp and followed. Whether the cloud stayed above the Tabernacle for two days, a month, or a year, the people of Israel stayed in camp and did not move on. But as soon as it lifted, they broke camp and moved on. (Numbers 9:16–22 NLT)

For forty years in the wilderness, the Israelites were never alone and never lost. They had the most accurate guide ever. Their global positioning device was the almighty God who created the universe.

If someone's bladder awakened him in the middle of the night, no flashlight was needed, because God was acting as the biggest freaking night-light in history. No matter what time of day it was, the people could simply look to the giant pillar to be reminded that God was always with them, protecting them from danger and leading them at the proper pace to their ultimate destination.

Yet despite this twenty-four-hour, visible presence of the eternal God—the same God who provided daily food for them in the desert, who brought forth drinking water from a rock, who parted the Red Sea and allowed the Israelites to walk across on dry land—the people grumbled constantly, and in some cases rebelled openly against God. They worshipped a golden calf, complained about their food, and challenged the authority God had given to Moses.

So the next time you think you need a visible sign to strengthen your belief (or make you believe in God if you're an atheist), remember that God's very own people saw clear, physical manifestations of the Lord day and night for four straight decades—and were still rebellious.

Underwear That Didn't Vaporize

It's time to have some fun with a little science experiment.

First, take note of all the clothes you are wearing. (That is, of course, assuming you are wearing clothes right now. Between sunbathers, nudist colonies, and people who just like to be in the buff around the house, I guess I can't assume that everyone is clothed as they read this.)

But really, take a few moments to consider every piece of clothing you're wearing—your shirt, pants, dress, skirt, underwear, socks, even your shoes. Examine every inch of them, noting the color, any flaws, etc. Now feel the texture, letting your skin get in tune with how the fabric feels. Give them a good whiff, letting your sense of smell absorb the scent. If you didn't shower before reading this, do not blame me for any ill effects. And if anyone looks at you strangely, let him know you're working on a science experiment.

Now that you're really in touch with your clothing, you're ready for Phase Two. Now, wait forty years. That is the experiment. Wait forty long years, four entire decades, keeping all your clothing items and wearing them constantly. Wear them in the morning, midday, and afternoon. Go walking as much as possible in your shoes, especially in rough terrain, like the woods, mountains, or deserts.

Of course, I don't expect anyone to keep the same shoes or clothing for the next forty years. If you're fifteen years old as you read this, you'd be fifty-five by the time the experiment is complete. If you're fifty now, you would be ninety when it's over.

Consider what your clothing would be like at the end of four decades—the everyday wear and tear, the standing, the sitting, the lying down, the walking, the running, the wiping of your hands on them (I can't be the only one who has that habit). You could even do laundry if you like.

Do you think your clothes would have the same color, texture, or scent? Do you think they would show signs of wearing out, if not being completely useless after such a long duration? Face it. Some people keep some of their clothing for so long, it's almost unwearable. It becomes like a dandelion. One good breeze will scatter any remaining thread molecules to the wind.

There is an amazing miracle tucked carefully away in the pages of Deuteronomy. It reveals that the clothes and shoes of the ancient Israelites did not suffer any physical wear and tear after *forty years* of exposure in the desert.

It's noted in just a single verse: "And I have led you forty years in the wilderness: your clothes are not waxen old upon you, and thy shoe is not waxen old upon thy foot" (29:5).

The New Living Translation puts it this way: "For forty years I led you through the wilderness, yet your clothes and sandals did not wear out."

The shoes did not wear out, and the underwear didn't vaporize!

The forty-year time period began when God led Moses and the twelve tribes of Israel out of Egypt, where they had been for exactly 430 years.

Even if the clothes and shoes they wore were brand-new on the day of the Exodus, it's still incredible that the shoes did not grow old as the people marched through the desert.

The desert has a harsh climate. It's hot and dry during daylight, and can get chilly at night. Clothes and shoes would wear out quickly there. Remember, the Israelites did not have the benefit of dry cleaners, Snuggle fabric softener, or even Calgon, the detergent with the "ancient Chinese secret." They had to rely on God for everything. And God took complete care of His people, even down to the smallest details of clothing and shoes. What a fantastic miracle!

The Egyptian Magicians

Believe it or not, some of the Bible's miracles appear to have come from "the dark side" instead of one of God's own agents. Case in point: the Egyptian magicians.

The magicians of the kingdom of Egypt performed amazing feats. They actually replicated the miracles God performed through Moses and his brother, Aaron, just before the Israelites marched out of captivity. These sun-worshipping sorcerers were thrust into the limelight when Moses arrived at the court of Egypt's pharaoh.

> And the LORD spake unto Moses and unto Aaron, saying, When Pharaoh shall speak unto you, saying, Shew a miracle for you: then thou shalt say unto Aaron, Take thy rod, and cast it before Pharaoh, and it shall become a serpent. And Moses and Aaron went in unto Pharaoh, and they did so as the LORD had commanded: and Aaron cast down his rod before Pharaoh, and before his servants, and it became a serpent. (Exodus 7:8–10)

This is not surprising. God indicated that the staff Aaron carried would become a snake when thrown to the ground, and that's exactly what happened. But in an interesting twist, the pagan priests of Egypt were able to duplicate the miracle.

> Then Pharaoh also called the wise men and the sorcerers: now the magicians of Egypt, they also did in like manner with their enchantments. For they cast down every man his rod, and they became serpents: but Aaron's rod swallowed up their rods. (vv. 11–12)

There is no indication that the Egyptian magicians had any difficulty turning their wooden rods into living creatures, but the result was certainly unexpected, as Aaron's rod, which had become a snake, went about swallowing up the "staff-snakes" of the sorcerers.

Where did these priests get the power to perform these magic tricks? Did their "enchantments" come from the devil? It is plausible that these men were worshippers of Satan, whether or not they called him by that title. The New Testament says that Satan does have power to perform miraculous events and give miracle-producing power to humans.

> And then shall that Wicked be revealed, whom the Lord shall consume with the spirit of his mouth, and shall destroy with the brightness of his

coming: even him, whose coming is after the working of Satan with all power and signs and lying wonders. (2 Thessalonians 2:8–9)

But as far as the Egyptian magicians are concerned, the Bible is not absolutely clear. The rest of the story could provide some clues.

First of all, the immediate reaction of the pharaoh was what the Bible terms a "hardened" heart: "And he hardened Pharaoh's heart, that he hearkened not unto them; as the LORD had said" (Exodus 7:13).

When God first dispatched Moses and Aaron to Pharaoh, he told them the king would be stiff-necked. God would need to take supernatural action to affect how Pharaoh would react.

And I will harden Pharaoh's heart, and multiply my signs and my won-ders in the land of Egypt. But Pharaoh shall not hearken unto you, that I may lay my hand upon Egypt, and bring forth mine armies, and my people the children of Israel, out of the land of Egypt by great judgments. (vv. 3–4)

It seems God was interested in not letting the people go too quickly or easily. He was looking for a buildup, so to speak, of miraculous events, so no one would doubt the true source of freedom for the Israelites.

The account then relates a list of plagues to be brought upon Egypt, starting with the waters of the nation turning to blood.

And the LORD spake unto Moses, Say unto Aaron, Take thy rod, and stretch out thine hand upon the waters of Egypt, upon their streams, upon their rivers, and upon their ponds, and upon all their pools of water, that they may become blood; and that there may be blood throughout all the land of Egypt, both in vessels of wood, and in vessels of stone. (v. 19)

The waters turned to blood, but, once again, the heathen wizards worked their magic and replicated the miracle: "And the magicians of Egypt did so with their enchantments: and Pharaoh's heart was hardened, neither did he hearken unto them; as the LORD had said" (v. 22).

Next came frogs. "And Aaron stretched out his hand over the waters of Egypt; and the frogs came up, and covered the land of Egypt. And the magicians did so with their enchantments, and brought up frogs upon the land of Egypt" (8:6–7).

But after the plague of frogs, something noteworthy occurred: the magicians were suddenly no longer able to copy the miracles.

> Aaron stretched out his hand with his rod, and smote the dust of the earth, and it became lice in man, and in beast; all the dust of the land became lice throughout all the land of Egypt. And the magicians did so with their enchantments to bring forth lice, but they could not: so there were lice upon man, and upon beast. (vv. 17–18)

The Scripture identifies the plague of lice as the turning point. Whether it was the devil granting them the power to perform miracles or God allowing it to happen, the ability of the Egyptian magicians ceased at this point. In fact, for the remaining plagues—flies, dying livestock, boils, hail, locusts, darkness, and the death of the firstborn—there is not even a hint that the magicians sought to copy the evils befalling their own people. Despite that, God continued to harden Pharaoh's heart until the final plague, the death of the firstborn of every living creature. It was so horrific that the Egyptians drove the Israelites from their presence, allowing them to take whatever riches they desired as they departed.

If the devil gave the Egyptian sorcerers the power to mimic Aaron, why did he stop? If God gave them the power, why? Was it to take it away from them and make them aware of their own shortcomings? The questions are interesting, but ultimately the Scriptures do not provide definitive answers.

Miracle of the Twilight Zone

There is one miracle in Scripture that reminds me of the 1960s television show *The Twilight Zone*. The specific episode from the series is titled "I Am the Night—Color Me Black," and deals with a town surrounded by pitch darkness even though the sun ought to have been shining. The story follows the slated execution of a man. The characters are filled with hate, which causes the mysterious envelope of blackness.

A similar event is recorded in the Old Testament. It does not have to do with dark clouds, or even a brief solar eclipse. The tenth chapter of Exodus recounts a three-day period of no light at all. There was only a "darkness which may be felt." It was actually the second-to-last plague on Egypt before the Israelites triumphantly marched out of captivity.

And the LORD said unto Moses, Stretch out thine hand toward heaven, that there may be darkness over the land of Egypt, even darkness which may be felt. And Moses stretched forth his hand toward heaven; and there was a thick darkness in all the land of Egypt three days. (vv. 21–22)

The Bible does not specify what, if any, physical cause prompted the darkness. It does not mention any unusual cloud movements or astronomical effects of celestial bodies. One may thus infer that the event was completely supernatural, especially since it lasted three entire days. More evidence suggesting it was supernatural is found in the verse that follows: "They saw not one another, neither rose any from his place for three days: but all the children of Israel had light in their dwellings" (v. 23).

The darkness was so black in Egypt that no one was able to see another person. It was like being blind. Everyone was forced to stay at home for seventy-two hours and wonder if they would ever see the brightness of the sun again. Egypt worshipped the sun, so it's no stretch to suggest that the people thought they had been abandoned by their own pagan god.

Even more mind-boggling is that while Egypt was shrouded in mysterious darkness, the conditions in the land of Goshen, where God's people resided, could not have been better. Their three-day forecast had plenty of sunshine, with no mention of extended periods of darkness. In the realm of physics, light does not stop at the county line, so to speak. It cannot be explained by some natural phenomenon. But while *The Twilight Zone* is sheer fiction, the ninth plague upon Egypt is the very dark truth of God.

The Day the Sun Stood Still

In 1951, a famous science fiction movie, *The Day the Earth Stood Still*, was released. But the film did not have anything to do with an event recorded in the Old Testament, when the rotation of the earth apparently stopped, halting the journey of the sun and moon across the sky.

The biblical account seems more like a scene from the 1978 film *Superman*. In that comic book tale brought to the silver screen, Superman was so upset by the death of his love interest, Lois Lane, that he flew against the earth's natural rotation. Though fanciful, the plan worked: the planet actually stopped spinning normally, having an impact on time.

In the Bible, time apparently came to a halt in a spectacular event that has never been repeated. It occurred in the book of Joshua, during a time when God was fighting the enemies of the Israelites. Joshua, Moses' successor and a prototype of Jesus Christ, was leading the people into the promised land.

> Then spake Joshua to the LORD in the day when the LORD delivered up the Amorites before the children of Israel, and he said in the sight of Israel, Sun, stand thou still upon Gibeon; and thou, Moon, in the valley of Ajalon. And the sun stood still, and the moon stayed, until the people had avenged themselves upon their enemies. Is not this written in the book of Jasher? So the sun stood still in the midst of heaven, and hasted not to go down about a whole day. And there was no day like that before it or after it, that the LORD hearkened unto the voice of a man: for the LORD fought for Israel. (10:12–14)

To make sure we are not missing anything hidden in the English of 1611, here's a modern version:

> On the day the Lord gave the Israelites victory over the Amorites, Joshua prayed to the Lord in front of all the people of Israel. He said, "Let the sun stand still over Gibeon, and the moon over the valley of Aijalon." So the sun and moon stood still until the Israelites had defeated their enemies. Is this event not recorded in [The Book of Jashar]? The sun stopped in the middle of the sky, and it did not set as on a normal day. The Lord fought for Israel that day. Never before or since has there been a day like that one, when the Lord answered such a request from a human being. (NLT)

One of my college professors of Old Testament history suggested that the Bible did not mean what it stated about the sun standing still. He said it was merely a poetic way of describing a full moon, which would give Joshua's army plenty of light to finish the job. There are some problems with such a theory, though.

First of all, the Scripture focuses on the movement of the celestial bodies, the sun and the moon, and the fact that their movement "stayed" and "stood still." It concerns neither the phase of the moon nor the amount of light it reflected for Joshua's army. It suggests instead that the rotation of the Earth could have been halted, thus freezing the positions of the sun and moon in the sky.

Second, this was not a nighttime event. It happened in daylight hours, and the sun "hasted not to go down about a whole day." So sunset was delayed for many hours.

Third, the book of Joshua, which is filled with military history and not poetry, emphasizes that the event was not a natural occurrence, such as a full moon, but a supernatural one—a direct result of Joshua's command. "And there was no day like that before it or after it, that the Lord hearkened unto the voice of a man: for the Lord fought for Israel."

Finally, would it not be within the ability of God to halt the rotation of the planet? After all, ask the Scriptures, "Is any thing too hard for the Lord?" (Genesis 18:14).

Even if the rotation had not been halted, there are other possibilities. It could have been a local phenomenon in that it appeared only to those in that specific location that the sun and moon stood still. Alternatively, God may have affected time itself. The Bible does not provide specifics, but does make it clear that God took action on behalf of Joshua to alter the length of the day.

One additional note: Scripture says this astounding event is also recorded in the book of Jasher. While Jasher is not part of the Bible, it still exists today. Here is the portion of that book that mentions the sun standing still:

And when they were smiting, the day was declining toward evening, and Joshua said in the sight of all the people, Sun, stand thou still upon Gibeon, and thou moon in the valley of Ajalon, until the nation shall have revenged itself upon its enemies. And the Lord hearkened to the voice of Joshua, and the sun stood still in the midst of the heavens, and it stood still six and thirty moments, and the moon also stood still and hastened not to go down a whole day. And there was no day like that, before it or after it, that the Lord hearkened to the voice of a man, for the Lord fought for Israel. (Jasher 88:63–65)

These miracles of the sun standing still, days of darkness for Egypt, nondeteriorating clothing, giant pillars of cloud and fire, immunity to snake venom, and long-distance exorcising provide only a small sampling of miracles in Scripture. Plenty more can be found when people actually crack open their Bibles and read what they may have never seen before, or simply have forgotten over time.

CONCLUSION

HOW MANY TIMES have you heard a newscaster give a report and then thought to yourself, *What nonsense!*? Misinformation and deception are rampant in our modern world. It's difficult to watch a newscast or pick up a paper without questioning the veracity of what's presented. And that's leaving aside the reporter's personal spin or bias.

But while many consumers of news are becoming more skeptical of what they see and hear these days, those who seek information about God or the Bible seem to rarely question what they're told. They often devour whatever they hear from family, friends, or fellow believers; accept it as the gospel; and toss in a "Praise the Lord," "Hallelujah," or "Amen, brother" for good measure.

I suggest it's time to examine everything you've ever been told about the Bible and see for yourself what it actually contains. Just as you can be skeptical of an offer that sounds too good to be true, or of news reports, why not challenge yourself to find out exactly *why* you believe what you believe?

For most people, this can be a difficult task. They don't wish to question the accepted beliefs and practices of society. After all, how could Mom and Dad have been wrong about what they taught me? How could my pastor or priest have been mistaken? How could millions of like-minded believers be in error? It's not easy to question what most people believe, even if most are basing their beliefs on fiction rather than fact. No one likes to rock the boat.

But no one outside of God is right about everything all the time. Not your mother and father, not your pastor or priest, and not the folks who said the Y2K bug would bring about the end of the world. If people really want to know what is in the Bible, then they need to find out for themselves.

At the end of the book of Ecclesiastes, King Solomon summarized life by stating, "Let us hear the conclusion of the whole matter: Fear God, and keep his commandments: for this is the whole duty of man" (12:13).

I could not agree more. Our duty as human beings is to fear God and follow the instructions He has provided for us.

But in order to do that, we need to make sure we have as much truth as possible about God and the commandments. After all, what good does it do to follow in error? All of us certainly want to follow the correct path, or at least I like to think most would want that. Throughout this book, I've tried to reveal faulty assumptions that people hold on to regarding God and the Bible. Some of these may have been personal assumptions, and some may have been the result of poor instruction. My intent is to point out that people assume far too much, but they can discover what's real if they take the time to investigate for themselves instead of relying on others. It's time to put away the fables and get back to facts.

For those who do seek truth, it is revealed in the pages of the Holy Bible. Many people already know that, but perhaps some were unaware of some of the amazing statements, events, and miracles they contain. Others may be unaware that the Bible does not mention some things they somehow thought were there all along. Regardless, everyone should at least be accurate when discussing the Bible's contents, and stop this nonsensical perpetuation of error.

I do not tell people what to think. What people believe is their own decision, and everyone has to make such decisions throughout his or her lifetime. I would venture to say, however, that most people can admit to changing their beliefs about something at some point. We are not born knowing everything. We all grow and mature, learning new things as we age. It's a very healthy process. But I think we should strive to base our beliefs and actions on correct information rather than falsehoods or misconceptions.

When Jesus Christ came to Earth as a human and lived more than three decades among us, He said many fantastic things and performed incredible miracles. He restored sight to blind people, enabled the lame to walk, and even resurrected people from the dead. While a few folks believed Jesus and changed their lives, most did not. To this day, there are more people on the planet who do not believe in the God of the Bible than those who do. This will only change after the return of Jesus, when the knowledge of God will cover the world.

Until that happens, the Bible says we are to fear God and keep His commandments. It's my hope that all readers of this book will discover that the real God of the Bible is even greater than previously thought.

Meanwhile, let me pose to you the same question once asked by the prophet Isaiah: "Who hath believed our report?" (53:1).